1935

CALGARY
An Illustrated History

The History of Canadian Cities

CALGARY
An Illustrated History

Max Foran

Photographs assembled by
Edward Cavell

James Lorimer & Company, Publishers
and
National Museum of Man,
National Museums of Canada

Toronto 1978

Copyright © 1978 by National Museums of Canada. Crown copyright reserved. No part of this book may be reproduced or transmitted in any form or by any means, electronic or mechanical, including photocopying, or by any information storage and retrieval system, without permission in writing from the publisher.

ISBN 0-88862-224-4 cloth

Design: Don Fernley
Cartography: Geoffrey J. Matthews
Printed and bound in Canada

Canadian Cataloguing in Publication Data

Foran, Max.
    Calgary

(The History of Canadian Cities)

ISBN 0-88862-224-4

1. Calgary, Alta. — History.   I. National Museum of Man.

II. Title. III. Series.

FC3697.4.F67   971.23′3   C78-001448-0
F1079.5.C35F67

James Lorimer & Company, Publishers
35 Britain Street
Toronto

Credits

Provincial Archives of Alberta: 172

Provincial Archives of Alberta (E. Brown Collection): 13, 15 (upper), 18, 19, 20, 21, 23, 29, 37, 41, 49, 51, 52, 62, 104

Provincial Archives of Alberta (H. Pollard Collection): 2, 31, 39, 46, 68, 81, 93, 121, 126, 127, 131, 133, 139, 160, 161, 162, 170

Glenbow-Alberta Institute: 14, 15 (lower), 26, 27, 33, 35, 38, 42, 43, 47, 53, 55, 57, 58, 59, 61, 63, 65, 69, 71, 72, 73, 75, 77, 78, 80, 83, 85, 87, 91, 94, 95, 97, 99, 101, 102, 103, 107, 108, 109, 111, 112, 114, 115, 119, 122, 136, 137, 140, 143, 144, 146, 147, 149, 150, 151, 153, 154, 169

Canadian Pacific Corporate Archives: 125

Edward Cavell: 173

Public Archives of Canada: 10 (C-1319)

Table of Contents

List of Maps

Appendix
List of Tables

Foreword
The History of Canadian Cities Series

The History of Canadian Cities Series is a project of the History Division, National Museum of Man (National Museums of Canada). The project was begun in 1977 in response to a continuing demand for more popular publications to complement the already well-established scholarly publication programs of the Museum. The purpose of this series is to offer the general public a stimulating insight into Canada's urban past. Over the next several years, the Museum, in co-operation with James Lorimer and Company, plans to publish a number of individual volumes dealing with such varied communities as Saint John and Vancouver, Regina and Montreal, Whitehorse and Ottawa.

It is the hope of the National Museum of Man that the publication of these books will provide the public with information on Canadian cities in an attractive, stimulating and readable form. At the same time, the plan of the series is to have authors follow a standard format and the result, it is anticipated, will be a systematic, interpretative and comprehensive account of the urban experience in many Canadian cities. Eventually, as new volumes are completed, *The History of Canadian Cities Series* will be a major step along the path to a general and comparative history of Canada's urban development.

The form chosen for this series — the individual urban biography — is based on the assumption that a community's history has meaning not discernible by a study of fragmentary portions only; that the totality of the urban experience is usually not present in thematic studies. Since the distinguishing feature of a good urban biography is the attempt to see the community as a whole and to relate the parts to a larger context, it was felt that the study of individual cities was at this time the best approach to an understanding of the Canadian urban experience.

In this volume, Max Foran provides a compelling story of the evolution of the City of Calgary from a tiny North West Mounted Police post in 1875 to one of Canada's most dynamic metropolitan centres in 1965. Max Foran is a Calgary school principal who has written many articles on the city's history. He received his B.Ed. and M.A. from the University of Calgary and is now completing his Ph.D. at the same institution.

Like other volumes in this series, the text has been enhanced by a fine collection of historical photographs that illustrate virtually all aspects of Calgary's history from its origins to the late 1960s. Edward Cavell, who assembled the photographs, is curator of photography at the Archives of the Canadian Rockies in Banff, Alberta.

Alan F. J. Artibise
General Editor

Already available in this series:
Winnipeg (published 1977)

Acknowledgements

I would like to thank the staff of the Glenbow-Alberta Institute for the many services rendered to me during the preparation of this book. In particular I would like to acknowledge the helpful assistance of archivists Sheilagh Jameson, Georgeen Barrass and Vicky Williams, who do much towards making the Glenbow such a pleasant place to work. I would also like to extend my thanks to Alan F. J. Artibise, general editor of this series, whose aid was much appreciated. Finally, I would like to thank my typist, Dierdre Slater, for her meritorious efforts in interpreting my original draft.

Max Foran
Calgary
June 1978

The Photographers

The settlement of Calgary and George Eastman's Kodak appeared almost simultaneously, and the ever-present camera has been an enduring feature of Calgary's history. When Fort Calgary was being built in the 1870s, photography had been maturing for almost 40 years. The originally cumbersome processes had been sufficiently simplified to pose few problems for surveyor-photographers travelling the frontier wilderness. Itinerant professional photographers followed civilization along the rails, ready to supply the folks back home with photographic proof that life in the new land really was prosperous and romantic. Some of these photographers remained in Calgary, and the documentation of a city was soon underway.

The photographs presented here are selected from the works of at least 30 professional photographers and an unknown number of amateurs. Of the professionals, three deserve special mention for the excellence of their work. One of the first major photographers in Calgary was W. H. Boorne, who photographed the city and western life in general from the late 1880s into the 1890s. His stunning images of city streets, new buildings, people (especially native people) and his marvelous ranching scenes form one of the earliest and most extensive records of pioneer life in the West. W. J. Oliver and Harry Pollard arrived in Calgary in the early years of this century. Their work exists as a fascinating record of the city's growth and development through the 1920s and '30s. Although they both maintained studios in Calgary, they also established national reputations. Oliver documented the national parks of Canada for the government, and Pollard travelled throughout the world as one of the principal photographers for the CPR. Both these men were consummate artists and left collections of beautifully made large-format negatives.

The works of professional photographers tend to reflect the more formal aspects of a society. In the early days, even images of people at work or play were rarely candid, since the photographer's bulky view camera was an obvious distraction. However, the Kodak (and its many imitators) revolutionized and humanized the photograph. The photographer could now be an unobtrusive family member, and the "snap shot" could reveal unpretentious moments of everyday life previously hidden from the non-participant. This book includes the warmth and intimacy of amateur photography as part of its documentation of Calgary's past.

Only a few of the thousands of photographs taken in and about Calgary during its first century are contained in this book. From the many images that have survived in various institutions and private collections, I have selected photographs on the basis of the strength and uniqueness of the image. I have also tried to show the technical excellence of most early photography. Hopefully these photographs capture part of the essence of Calgary.

Edward Cavell
Banff
June 1978

One of the earliest North West Mounted Police encampments on the site of what is now Calgary. A division of the recently established Mounted Police reached the confluence of the Bow and Elbow Rivers late in the summer of 1875, and by the autumn a rudimentary Fort Calgary stood at that location.

Introduction

The Origins of Calgary 1875-1884

Fur brought the white man to the Canadian West. In his relentless pursuit of pelts he spread his mantle of influence across the northern reaches of Canada. His canoes carried him up the cold, broad rivers where he built forts, formed his fragile Indian alliances and perpetuated the growing legend of a harsh, forbidding land that invited no one except the hunters of the beaver. Rocky Mountain House, established in 1799 on the North Saskatchewan River, marked the most successful southernmost penetration of the fur trade in Alberta, and until approximately 1850 the area around Calgary was little marred by the tracks of the few white men who, under the threat of rival competition, restlessly probed the mountain barrier seeking fresh sources and new routes.

Settlement of the Canadian West began in 1869 when Britain finally persuaded her reluctant former colony to take possession of Rupert's Land. Long the exclusive preserve of the Hudson's Bay Company, this vast, forbidding area had assumed international importance in imperial politics. The vulnerability of western Canada was underscored by Britain's fears of unrestrained American expansion and the emergence of the north Pacific as a focus of international interest. The newly formed Canadian government purchased Rupert's Land for a transfer price of £300,000 and, five years later, established the North West Mounted Police to guard the newly acquired territory. In their historic 1874 march from Fort Dufferin, the North West Mounted Police sounded the death knell of an old order.[1] Lawlessness, white transience and the autonomy of native people slowly gave way to the agricultural frontier of permanent settlement.

The North West Mounted Police came to southern Alberta in the summer of 1874 to protect the native people from whisky traders. These men had operated on the infamous Whoop-Up Trail, extending from Fort Benton, Montana to a string of illegal posts in southern Alberta.[2] Fort Macleod was established in the fall of 1874, and its presence pushed the whisky traders farther into Blackfoot country. Calgary therefore originated as part of the NWMP's plans to establish a network of posts in Indian territory. It was apparent by the winter of 1874-75 that a post was needed in the Bow River area, but the precise reasons for locating the fort at the confluence of the Bow and Elbow Rivers are conjectural.

The Blackfoot, Sarcee and Stoney tribes were concentrated in large numbers in the Bow and Elbow River valleys. The swift-flowing Bow, which often remained partially unfrozen, attracted wintering buffalo, and the high river banks afforded excellent protection from biting winter winds. The establishment of Fort Macleod did not, however, deter the whisky traders in this area; they still found it easy to evade the police and slip across the United States border. Accordingly, on April 10, 1875, an order in council was passed in Ottawa authorizing the construction of a fort on the Bow River. The exact spot was chosen in the summer of 1875 when a police officer and guide visited the area and staked a buffalo robe in the vicinity of the present-day Holy Cross Hospital. The Reverend John McDougall, who in 1873 had established a Methodist mission at Morley, 40 miles west of Calgary, later maintained that it was he who had suggested the spot to Colonel Macleod. McDougall probably knew the country as well as any white man, and certainly his opinion would have carried some weight with Macleod. In any case, it is fairly certain that Inspector Ephrem A. Brisebois received instructions to locate the new post near the confluence of the Bow and Elbow Rivers. When his division returned from the Red Deer River, where it had met with the touring general of the Canadian militia, Sir Edward Selby-Smith, they forded the Bow River from the north, and this probably explains why the post was located right at the confluence of the two rivers rather than the spot marked by the buffalo robe about a mile to the south.

The exact date of the arrival of the police is not known, as early records of the North West Mounted Police were destroyed by fire in 1897. Although an officer with the original F Troop later claimed that they arrived in early September 1875, historian Hugh Dempsey has suggested late August as a more likely date.[3] Naming the new post also provoked a dispute. Commanding officer Ephrem Brisebois initially named the fort after himself. However, Brisebois' later misuse of authority earned him the disfavour of his superiors, and after rebellious acts by the men of F Troop in the winter of 1875-76, Brisebois was considered unfit to command. A new name was chosen for the fort in January 1876, and eight months later Brisebois, his military reputation ruined, resigned from the force. "Calgary's forgotten founder" died in obscurity in 1890 at the age of 39.[4] Colonel James Macleod's choice of the Scottish "Calgary" as a name for the new post was approved, and given the accepted translation of "clear running water", it certainly seemed an appropriate name for a fort that stood beside two swiftly flowing streams. However, historian George F.G. Stanley has proven that "Calgary" derives from a Gaelic form meaning "bay farm" or "bay pasture".[5]

A rudimentary Fort Calgary was built in the fall of 1875 from spruce and pine logs cut upstream and floated down the Elbow River. Pole roofs were covered with earth, logs were chinked with clay, and the floors were bare earth. Besides quarters for the men, a guard room, stables and storage facilities, a separate section for officers was also erected. Fort Calgary was completed in time to celebrate a Christmas dinner given by the non-commissioned officers for the local residents.

Calgary was essentially a creation of the federal government. The establishment of the fort ensured the physical presence of government authority and provided a focal point for social and economic activity. Within weeks of the erection of Fort Calgary, two trading companies established posts. The I.G. Baker Company of Montana, the major trading establishment in the region, constructed Fort Calgary for $2,476 before building its post a few

hundred yards away. Soon after, the Hudson's Bay Company moved its post down the Bow from the Ghost River to locate on the east bank of the Elbow opposite the fort. The traders were soon joined by Methodist and Roman Catholic missionaries who conducted regular services.

During these early years, Fort Calgary existed primarily to maintain Ottawa's concepts of law and order among the native people, while the missionaries in and around Calgary also attempted to convert them. After the 1877 signing of Treaty No. 7, the mobility of the native people was strictly limited, and in the next decade they provided trade and low-paid services vital to the continued existence of the fort. But by 1881, the settlement of Fort Calgary had begun to undermine the native culture far more drastically than the whisky traders had. As the result of white contact, prostitution, begging and petty thievery were common. The number of tepees surrounding the settlement increased steadily and indicated the native people's growing dependence on white culture.

The slaughter and eventual disappearance of the buffalo in the late 1870s marked the end of an era. Both Calgary and the native people were affected severely by the loss of this valuable resource. Trade slackened, and in 1879 the Hudson's Bay Company considered abandoning its post. Money was scarce, and prices for staples, always high, became exorbitant. Furthermore, the homesteaders found it difficult to raise crops on a consistent basis. In 1880, starving Sarcees from the local reserve, who were not receiving the food supplies promised in their treaty with the government, threatened the settlement. Although the Mounted Police suppressed them swiftly and without bloodshed, it was obvious that after five years of existence inadequate provision for the well-being of the native people was making Fort Calgary's position precarious.

Yet it was the disappearance of the buffalo which made possible an open-range cattle industry. Buffalo and cattle could not co-exist, because the bison would kill the bulls and take the cows into the herd. In 1880, pressured by British and Canadian capital, the government took advantage of the recent removal of import duties on cattle from the United States to introduce a controversial lease system. Long-term leases of up to 100,000 acres per year brought an influx of men and money onto the open range. The

(169) MUTSINAMAKAN & SQUAW, SARCEE INDIANS. C.W. MATHERS EDMONTON N.W.T. CAN.

In the decade after 1875, the nomadic hunting patterns of native people and white hunters were disrupted by permanent settlement in the West, and the fur and buffalo trade was replaced by commercial livestock raising. For centuries, native people like these Sarcees had relied on the buffalo herds for almost all their needs. But the white man slaughtered the animals for profit and sport. With the loss of the buffalo, native people were forced to relinquish traditional ways of life and, restricted to reserves, were expected to become farmers overnight.

In the early 1880s, Calgary was a collection of tents, log buildings and wooden shacks. The more substantial structures of the "sandstone era" did not begin to appear until later in the decade.

Most of the commercial buildings in early Calgary were one-storey structures built up to the street line, with straight fronts and large signs.

Many early businessmen lived in the rear of their stores or in small houses built nearby. This scene shows Eighth Avenue in 1884.

first major herd of 3,000 cattle crossed the Bow River near present-day Mewata Park in 1881 on its way to Cochrane. By the end of 1883, there were over 25,000 head of cattle between the Bow River and the American boundary, and a year later, 1.7 million acres were under lease to 41 companies.[6] Southern Alberta had become cattle country.

The introduction of the cattle industry had immediate ramifications for Calgary. The surrounding district attracted settlers, most of whom were drawn by the promise of successful stock-raising. By 1883, about 40 people occupied 18 of the 36 sections which formed the city of Calgary in 1912. The Cochrane Ranch Company opened a butcher's shop in Calgary within a month of the arrival of the first herd in 1881. However, Calgary did not become the first centre of the livestock industry. As long as the north-south transportation route operated, Fort Macleod's location remained superior to Calgary's in relation to the southern Alberta ranchlands.

Calgary's role as a transportation centre was re-defined and consolidated by the momentous decision in the spring of 1881 to re-route the Canadian Pacific Railway across the prairies, rather than following the North Saskatchewan River valley through Battleford and Fort Edmonton. This decision was in part influenced by Professor John Macoun, a naturalist with the Dominion government. In his three visits to the Northwest, Macoun was the first professional with first-hand experience to speak optimistically about the agricultural potential of the Canadian plains. He was particularly impressed with the Bow River valley, and when he visited Calgary in 1879, he wrote glowingly of its future.[7]

In 1881, advance parties of CPR engineers ran preliminary lines through the Bow River valley, and in 1882 Calgary was made supply headquarters for the expeditions seeking a mountain pass over the Rockies. True to tradition, the CPR kept secret its decision about Fort Calgary, and as late as March 1883 there were rumours that the rails would pass a few miles to the north through Nose Creek. Despite the rumours, most people seemed confident that the CPR would come to Fort Calgary. In addition to the security of the law, the railway men were particularly impressed with the potential of section 15 immediately west of the fort as a potential townsite. This section was railway land under terms of contract and, according to Superintendent James

Egan, "a natural townsite and far ahead of any location that we have on the line of the road".[8] Like the native people and the North West Mounted Police before them, the railway men were drawn to the confluence of the Bow and Elbow Rivers as a natural place for people to congregate.

The promise of the railroad changed Calgary from a police post to a potential urban centre. A wide variety of businessmen began arriving in 1881, and by the time the rails arrived in August 1883 about 40 merchants squatted around the fort on both sides of the unbridged Elbow River. As long as land titles were uncertain or the location of the railway station remained vague, newcomers refused to construct permanent dwellings. Calgary was a tent and shack town.

Economically, these were good years. The railway construction crews spent freely in Calgary. Contractors in charge of railway construction filled some of their orders in Calgary. Local butchers supplied enormous quantities of fresh meat to construction crews. In 1883, the Silver City strike west of Banff excited interest in the mineral potential of the Rocky Mountains. Many prospectors were outfitted in Calgary. Ranching supplies and equipment were also purchased. Bath houses, billiard halls and saloons were popular attractions, as were the inevitable bordellos and spontaneous gambling contests. In the months preceding and following the arrival of the rails, prices rose and business boomed. George Murdoch, a harnessmaker from New Brunswick who became Calgary's first mayor, admitted that he "charged like mischief".[9] It was in this atmosphere of plentiful money and high demand that some of Calgary's businessmen laid the foundations of their later prosperity.

On August 9, 1883, the rails reached the east bank of the Bow River, and two days later engines "Old 81" and "126" brought the first train of eight boarding and sixteen flat cars into Calgary. Following the construction of a bridge across the Elbow River, a temporary station was constructed in the vicinity of Fourth Street East. The construction crew pitched camp near the present location of the Capitol Theatre. Later, a water tank and a windmill were erected on the banks of the Elbow.[10] Although a regular train service did not begin until 1886, the creation of this east-west transportation link revitalized the town.

The pattern for Calgary's physical growth was set in January

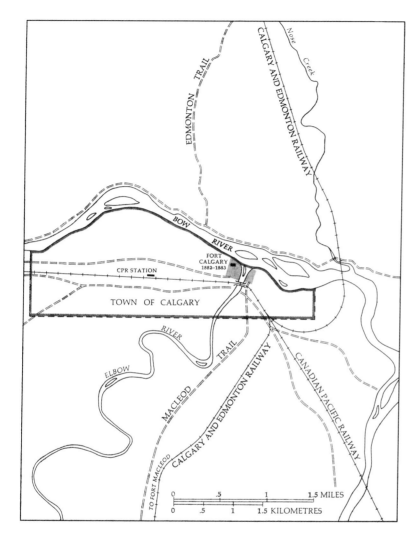

1 Calgary in 1884

1884, when the CPR chose its station site and offered the first sale of townsite lots. The controversy surrounding this particular decision showed the early implications of land speculation in

shaping eventual land-usage patterns in Calgary. The shack and tent town which had clustered under the protective wing of the law prior to the arrival of the rails was concentrated on both sides of the Elbow River. This area was designated government land open to homestead entry, and in normal circumstances would not be considered by the CPR for townsite purposes. However, the odd-numbered section immediately west of the fort, although ostensibly CPR land under terms of contract, was of uncertain status. The North West Mounted Police utilized the area for pasturage, and there were hints that the federal government would pre-empt the section. Many felt that the railway would then be compelled to locate its station and townsite to take in the existing settlement, particularly if a sizeable number of residents had permanent title to land.

In September 1882, the federal government acted. It created a reserve on section 15 west of the fort, maintaining that the expanded police post required permanent pasturage. The Mounted Police were instructed to prevent building on this section, forcibly if necessary.[11] It is difficult to ascertain whether the government was acting in its own interests or in those of the CPR. Around this time the CPR had disclosed plans for a possible route north of the Bow River. It appears more than coincidental that the government would reserve additional land across the river on the probable right-of-way. The government may have been anticipating its own townsite with substantial land sale revenues. On the other hand, it may have been guarding CPR interests by preventing squatting.

When the rails arrived, the ownership of section 14 was equally uncertain. In the late 1870s, employees of the Hudson's Bay Company were allowed to build permanent dwellings and break land on this section. Indeed, their actions were under the auspices of the Hudson's Bay Company, which at that time was considering its own withdrawal from the area.[12] But when Louis Rozelle made application for homestead entry to the southwest quarter of this section in late 1882, this action was contested by the Hudson's Bay Company, whose attitude of benign indifference had changed dramatically with news of the coming railroad. The company claimed the whole section under terms of the 1869 Rupert's Land transfer and made known its intention to acquire land north of the Bow River under the same authority.[13] Like the

COPYRIGHT
ERNEST BROWN.
738

CALGARY 1883.

"HERALD" BLDG.

COPYRIGHT
ERNEST BROWN

R.C. MISSION CALGARY, 1883.

№ 736

The Roman Catholic mission of ''Our Lady of Peace'' was first established in the early 1870s. This structure was built in 1882-83.

OPPOSITE PAGE: The Calgary Herald *building (far right) was one of the major structures in early Calgary. Founded by two Ontarioans, Andrew Moorhead Armour and Thomas Bernard Braden, the* Herald *played an important role in ''boosting'' the town's fortunes. In its first issue of August 31, 1883, the newspaper announced that ''Calgary has long been acknowledged as the great central point of the extensive fertile strip along the Rockies . . . but it will now assume a place of much more importance, and will become the greatest distributing point west of Winnipeg.''*

Throughout its history, Calgary has cultivated a "cowtown" image. Ranching was especially important to local economic life in the 1880s and 1890s, when the agricultural potential of the prairies seemed doubtful. Ranchers invested in local commerce and industry and were involved in the formation of Calgary's first manufacturing establishments.

(1013.) RANCHING SCENE IN ALBERTA, CATTLE BRANDING. 1884.

Branding cattle, 1884.

federal government, the Hudson's Bay Company was taking no chances in anticipating the railroad route through the Bow River valley. The claim was still unsettled by late summer 1883, when Rozelle transferred his right to the quarter to absentee eastern Canadian land speculators. These men had apparently bought Rozelle out for $10,000 on the advice of senior Conservative politicians who had assured them of the legitimacy of Rozelle's claim and of the government's favourable attitude towards a section 14 townsite.[14]

The end result was never in doubt. The CPR held the advantage. Since no clear title could be issued to land on section 14 pending settlement of the claim, there was no nucleus of permanently settled residents to influence the railway's decision. The government eventually backed down on the pasturage issue, and in December 1883 railway surveyors laid out the townsite about three-quarters of a mile west of the fort. The station was erected on the north side of the tracks, and the first sale of townsite lots was offered to prospective buyers.

It is probable that, despite the efforts of the federal government, the Hudson's Bay Company and the land speculators, the CPR would have created its section 15 townsite. Certainly, senior officials with the company had indicated their desire to act independently of any dispute on section 14. However, Calgary presented a different situation from many of the other towns created along the mainline. With almost a decade of settlement before the arrival of the rails, Calgary residents felt strongly independent and determined to resist the CPR and its well-known disregard for individual wishes. The actions of the Hudson's Bay Company delayed the issuance of clear title to land on section 14. Similarly, by prohibiting squatting on section 15, the federal government prevented a fringe settlement on the eastern boundary of the same section. But the CPR, with an empty section at its disposal and about 200 landless merchants eager to begin permanent business, was able to act arbitrarily and place its station well beyond the nucleus of the existing settlement (see Map 1).

The town of Calgary emerged on section 15 during the winter of 1883-84. At the first sale of townsite lots in January 1884, 185 out of 188 were located east along Atlantic (Ninth) and Stephen (Eighth) Avenues, within three blocks of the railway station. Businessmen skidded their dwellings across the frozen Elbow

River to take advantage of the Canadian Northwest Land Company's generous offer of 50 per cent rebates on lots purchased if buildings were erected before April 1. By spring, there was a sufficient sense of permanence to encourage town incorporation.

Incorporation was a pragmatic issue. Taxation revenues were needed to supply essential services, especially fire prevention.[15] The flimsy clapboard buildings which comprised much of Calgary were fire traps, and owners faced exorbitant fire insurance rates. A town fire brigade would reduce the hazard and lower the premiums. In January 1884, a Citizens' Committee was elected to work for town incorporation, and an application to the legislature of the Northwest Territories was prepared during the spring and summer of 1884. Frequent meetings were held in James Reilly's Royal Hotel, a tinderbox fabricated from the portable houses Reilly used to sell to CPR contractors before he made Calgary his home. Located on the corner of Stephen Avenue and Mactavish (Centre) Street, this three-storey hotel was regarded as the finest west of Winnipeg despite the fact that the upper portion was partitioned into male and female quarters by cotton sheets. Reilly had had experience in incorporation matters, having been part of a group which promoted the incorporation of Regina in 1883. Among those elected to the seven-member Calgary committee were George Clift King, long-time postmaster and the Mountie who first forded the Bow River in 1875, and James Walker, another ex-NWMP member who, as committee chairman, became Calgary's first unofficial mayor.

The movement for town incorporation was spearheaded by a few energetic businessmen, but the $500 incorporation fee was not raised easily. Several landholders on section 14 east of the Elbow River were hostile to the idea. In late 1883, with the invalidation of the Hudson's Bay Company's claim, the crucial quarter of section 14 was legally owned by eastern Canadian land speculators. After failing to retain the nucleus of settlement east of the Elbow, these individuals attempted to delay and then change the terms of incorporation to exclude section 14. The settlement was again sharply divided, with some businessmen east of the Elbow River maintaining that they would receive no material advantages from incorporation. To members of the Citizens' Committee, however, the eastern Canadian speculators were the real villains. George Murdoch referred to them as "east-

(947) PLOUGHING SCENE, NR CALGARY. 1884.

BOORNE & MAY, CALGARY, N. W. T.

COPYRIGHT
ERNEST BROWN

After the introduction of range cattle in the 1880s, southern Alberta's reputation as ranching country was firmly established. For years rangemen resisted the encroaching agricultural frontier, maintaining that climatic conditions were not conducive to intensive crop farming. They also feared the possible disappearance of the natural grass cover which was ideal for grazing and would be lost forever if broken for sod. The ranchers' fears proved all too true. Particularly in southeastern Alberta, crops failed to thrive on land where "prairie wool" had once supported domestic cattle and buffalo herds.

ern vampires who come here, invest nothing and try to get out of paying taxes".[16] The attitude of the CPR also presented problems to those working for incorporation. Experience in Regina had already revealed that the railway company, through its subsidiary the Canadian Northwest Land Company, had no intention of paying municipal taxes to the towns it created. Clearly, the taxation burden would rest on the shoulders of a few people. It is thus not surprising that the initial enthusiasm which surrounded the election of the Citizens' Committee in January 1884 had waned considerably by the summer.

But in November 1884, the committee proved successful. Calgary was incorporated as the second town in the Northwest Territories. When George Murdoch received the telegraphed message, he fired his gun, signalling the news to all within earshot. Later, a torchlight procession and other festivities celebrated the occasion. The subsequent civic election was a lively affair, and in 1885 the irrepressible George Murdoch began his tenure as Calgary's first mayor.

The incorporation of Calgary came under the 1883 Northwest Territories Municipal Ordinance, No. 2. Borrowed largely from Ontario municipal law, this ordinance defined the nature of the franchise and provided for sources of revenue and borrowing limits. The reliance on the property tax to establish the mill rate had two wide-reaching effects. First, it ensured the continued restriction of the municipal franchise at the expense of renters, tenants and those without property. Secondly, it affirmed the governing right of property, specifically represented by the merchants. Local government was very much a businessman's preserve.[17]

By the time Calgary was incorporated, it had already assumed responsibilities inherent in town and country relationships. Regular mail service to areas north and south of the mainline emanated from Calgary. The major religious denominations built permanent churches in 1883-84 and provided services to the surrounding district. On August 31, 1883, Calgary's first newspaper appeared. Elaborately labelled the *Calgary Herald, Mining and Ranch Advocate and General Advertiser*, the *Herald*, as it came to be known, was the voice of an important triumvirate who guided Calgary's early development and ardently supported the policies of the federal Conservative Party, the CPR and the ranching

industry. During the winter of 1883-84, attempts were made to establish banking services in Calgary, but the much advertised Ranchers' Bank failed to materialize. Federal government officials responsible for regional management of homestead entries, mining, timber and immigration were also stationed in the town by 1884.

The local initiative which resulted in the incorporation of Calgary manifested itself in other areas as local residents began to organize the town's institutional growth. Calgary's first masonic order, the Bow River Lodge, was established in 1883 in George Murdoch's shack. By early 1884, a literary society was in existence. Steps were taken in 1884 to form an agricultural society; meetings were held to establish Calgary as a school district; and public subscription raised the funds necessary to erect a footbridge across the Elbow River. Petitions regarding construction of roads and bridges were forwarded to the territorial and federal governments. Provisions were made for cemetery requirements. Church congregations organized themselves into formal bodies and prepared plans for buildings and permanent ministers.

Leadership in these activities came from the same individuals who had organized the Citizens' Committee. Most of these men were intending to stay in Calgary. George Murdoch brought the bulk of his personal wealth to Calgary with him. He, like many others, readily invested in both town and district property. These men were quick to realize that their own material success and personal well-being would be enhanced by the establishment of vital economic and social organizations. Regardless of the size and nature of their businesses, the merchants comprised the only group large and cohesive enough to begin laying the foundations for urban life.

When Calgary began its municipal life, it included those portions of sections 14, 15 and 16 south of the Bow River. Only the first two were occupied commercially, and indeed the town was little more than a collection of ramshackle dwellings strung out in an east-west direction north of the tracks. Almost all businesses, retail and otherwise, catered to the everyday needs of a predominantly male population. There were few facilities to indicate the town's anticipated role as marketing and distributing centre. The ribbon of steel which had ensured Calgary's continued survival had not yet begun to tap the wealth of the hinterland.

Chapter One

Frontier Town
1885-1905

Calgary consolidated its position as the most important distributing centre for southern Alberta in the two decades following incorporation. Further railway construction enhanced the town's location, and the ranching industry stimulated internal growth and district development. In its efforts to attract people and capital to the West, Calgary, through the inveterate optimism of its boosters, became regional spokesman. Indeed, the common aspirations of town and country were most observable during these years of modest economic expansion.

ECONOMIC GROWTH AND METROPOLITAN DEVELOPMENT

The railway was crucial to Calgary's economic development. As early as 1884, the *Herald* saw Calgary as a potential rival to the American railway-livestock centre, Chicago:

> We do not pretend to the role of prophet yet it requires little foresight to predict that the City of Calgary will be the largest in the North-West Territories. We already anticipate another Chicago and can hear the sound of the busy mill or see in the mind's eye the street cars plying their traffic from east of 14 to west of 16 and from river to river in the opposite direction.[1]

Over the years, local promoters continued to compare Calgary with Chicago rather than with Winnipeg, the metropolis of western Canada. The laying of rails to Edmonton in 1891-92 and to Fort Macleod two years later gave Calgary the four-way traffic it needed to ensure regional dominance. Calgary became the first wholesale centre in Alberta, with spur lines running to the various warehouses that began to appear along Tenth Avenue.

Heavy agricultural equipment was purchased in Calgary and transported to newly settled areas north of the city in the 1890s. The small urban centres along the newly constructed lines turned to Calgary for many of their supplies. The slackening of Calgary's retail trade in the mid 1890s was attributed to increased competition from smaller towns and indicated Calgary's widening wholesale function. The construction of the Crow's Nest branch of the CPR in 1897 gave Calgary access to the coking ovens, mining and lumber camps of the East Kootenai, which also provided a ready market for livestock products. In 1898, city council persuaded the CPR to locate freight yard facilities in Calgary. Federal government agencies established district offices in Calgary, and issues of justice, timber and grazing leases, homestead entries and immigration were arbitrated and acted upon by officials resident in Calgary. By the turn of the century, the railway had ensured the continuing survival of Calgary as a distributing and administrative centre for an extensive, largely non-agricultural hinterland.

The railway did not, however, induce major settlement. Even the most ardent promotional efforts could not disguise the failure of agriculture in the West. This lack of success was particularly noticeable in the Calgary district, where considerable acreage was already under grazing leases. Despite strenuous efforts by the Calgary Agricultural Society to promote grain growing, the Calgary district lagged far behind the Edmonton area in wheat and barley cultivation. Homestead entries did not increase steadily between 1885-1896, and the commercial emphasis was on livestock. In 1888, Calgary imported 300 barrels of flour, while in 1892 it was estimated that it cost the town $85,000 a year to import flour.[2] The dry years of the early 1890s aggravated matters fur-

In 1884, the Hudson's Bay Company facilities were moved from a trading post called Bow River Fort to this store in east Calgary.

Stores on Eighth Avenue, c. 1900.

Worden Brothers' Bakery on Eighth Avenue, 1900.

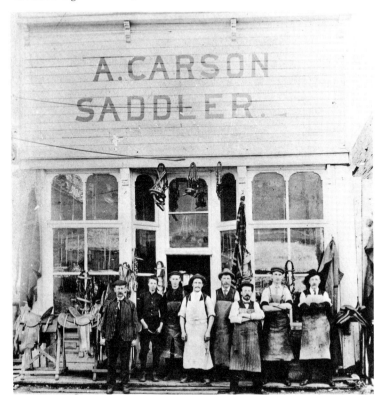

Employees of A. Carson's Calgary Saddlery Company, Eighth Avenue, 1900.

The Bain Stables stood opposite the CPR station on Ninth Avenue.

ther, and by 1895 it seemed increasingly unlikely that grain would ever be grown in commercial quantities in the Calgary district. The town council's assiduous lobby for an experimental farm in 1892 was partly in hopes of solving crop-growing problems.[3] Rancher Alfred Ernest Cross referred to the inevitable failure of profitable crop-raising as late as 1896-97, when, following successive years of summer frosts, dry seasons and low prices, "one could see numerous places abandoned, and allowed to go to waste, buildings tumbled down, fence posts rotted and barb wire strewn about the prairie".[4] In the 1890s the Calgary council had trouble securing a grain milling operation for the town. Local authorities considered municipal ownership before offering $3,000, a free site and tax exemptions for 10 years to anyone who would build and operate a flour mill.[5] When an Ontario man finally accepted the council's proposal in 1892, he was forced to purchase wheat from Moose Jaw in order to keep his operations at full capacity.[6]

The failure of commercial crop-raising before 1900 emphasized Calgary's reliance on the livestock industry and affected population growth in surrounding rural areas. In the 1901 census, towns like Airdrie, Acme, Crossfield, Strathmore and Langdon were not mentioned, while the combined populations of High River, Didsbury and Okotoks numbered only 618.

The coming of the railway to Calgary defeated Fort Macleod's hopes of retaining its position as headquarters of the cattle industry. Calgary assumed this role in 1887-88 with the first cattle shipments to Great Britain. In 1886, town authorities persuaded the CPR to build stockyards on section 11 just outside the town limits where "the prevailing winds would not carry the offensive effluvia from the yards over the town".[7] Five thousand head were sold on the British market in 1888 at prices between $40 and $50 per head, and over the next decade shipments to Canadian markets contributed substantially to the district's economic growth. The British Columbia market was particularly profitable. Over a half million pounds of dressed beef were shipped from Calgary to interior British Columbia in 1897, while five years later almost 10,000 head of stock were marketed in the Pacific province. By 1902, however, the peak years had been reached, and the future of the cattle industry, as it then existed, was in doubt.

Many factors retarded the growth of the cattle industry.[8] Large lease holdings allowed little control over breeding and, with the importation of inferior stock, resulted in poorer quality animals for export. The first provincial bull sale held in Calgary in 1901 represented an attempt to upgrade breeding stock. Vagaries of weather and disease on range-fed cattle militated further against consistent growth. The winter of 1886-87 was catastrophic. Stock losses were estimated at 50 to 60 per cent. An outbreak of pleuro-pneumonia in the early 1890s resulted in a British embargo on Alberta beef. Mange in cattle contributed to heavy losses in the late 1890s and further undermined confidence in open-range operations. Liberal Party policies after 1896, such as reluctance to implement policies for the managed use of unalienated government lands, were also considered detrimental to the cattle industry.

Calgary remained primarily a shipping point for livestock. Exports of dead meat to eastern markets were negligible. Inadequate refrigeration and reasonable freight rates on livestock shipments combined to create local and regional markets for Calgary's dressed meat products. The healthy nature of these markets stimulated Calgary's economy and gave rise to the city's first bona fide millionaire, Pat Burns. More than anyone else, Burns gave substance to the city's role as the centre of the livestock industry.[9] While other meatworks and associated businesses existed in Calgary before and after his arrival in 1890, Burns was the only person able to provide operations large enough to promote Calgary on a national scale. Burns' comment in 1912 that he had "made Calgary"[10] was not without some foundation.

Burns' legendary rags-to-riches story claims that he walked most of the way from his homestead in Minnedosa to Winnipeg in 1886. He was unprepossessing, chubby and uneducated, but had an excellent eye for cattle and opportunity. He came west in the 1880s with the railway construction crews of Mackenzie and Mann and filled beef contracts in Saskatchewan before reaching Calgary in 1890. From a small slaughterhouse in east Calgary, he supplied beef to construction workers on the Calgary-to-Edmonton line. In the next decade he opened the British Columbia market, floated cattle down the Yukon and simultaneously met local demands for beef. By 1899, Burns had expanded beyond the distributing and marketing business and had entered the beef-

The American-owned Eau Claire Lumber Company began business in 1886. Its mill, shown here in 1892, was located on the Bow River near the present Centre Street Bridge. Directed by Canadians Peter Prince and Isaac K. Kerr, the company was by the early 1890s the largest producer of lumber in the Northwest Territories.

packing industry. His Pacific trade in that year was estimated at $1.5 million. Extensive facilities were built in Calgary, his head office. In 1902, Burns began experimenting with summer deliveries of frozen dressed meats and in July shipped 400 head of dressed cattle wrapped in cotton and burlap to Vancouver. By 1905, Burns' meat enterprises had made Calgary the headquarters of a western Canadian beef-packing industry.

Burns' success depended on his willingness to gamble on regional markets. He had been so confident of the British Columbia market that, in 1897, he offered to buy every available head in southern Alberta. In 1902, he began to put a stranglehold on the western Canadian market by acquiring the holdings of William Roper Hull, also of Calgary and owner of extensive abattoir facilities and several retail outlets in Alberta and British Columbia. Burns attempted to control all phases of production from owning his own breeding herds to selling the finished table product. The *Herald* referred to Burns' organization in 1899 as "the most efficient distributing plant on the continent of America in the hands of an individual or firm".[11]

The influence of the cattle industry on Calgary was not confined to Pat Burns. Ranching capital was instrumental in establishing most of Calgary's manufacturing concerns throughout this period (Appendix, Table I). One of the most important was the Calgary Brewing and Malting Company, formed in 1892 by Alfred Ernest Cross, William Roper Hull and John Lineham. Ranching money was also invested in a tannery, soapworks and cold storage facilities in the 1890s. George Alexander, who constructed Calgary's first waterworks in 1889, had ranching connections. Similarly, many of the handsome sandstone commercial blocks built before the turn of the century were financed by ranching capital. Of these, the most notable was the elaborate Alberta Hotel, the favourite meeting place for Calgary's most colourful characters. In 1891, when the controlling interests in this impressive hotel incorporated themselves into a company with a capital stock of $99,000, ranching interests provided the chief stockholders.[12] Ranchers invested in town real estate and local commercial recreational organizations and were prominent on the boards of directors of mining and railway companies formed in Calgary before 1900. During these years, Calgary truly was a "cowtown".

By 1905, ranching had given Calgary a livestock trade and a meat-packing industry catering mainly to regional demands. There were indications, however, that difficult years might be ahead for both. American meat-packing firms like Swift and Armour were developing refrigeration techniques and were already establishing western Canadian outposts. The importation of high-quality refrigerated meat was making it difficult to distinguish chilled from freshly killed beef. Calgary's dependence on the ranching industry was vulnerable to all these developments.

The railway gave an initial advantage to other enterprising Calgary businessmen. James Walker was joined in the lumber business in 1886 by the American-owned Eau Claire Lumber Company. Directed by Canadians Peter Prince and Isaac K. Kerr, the Eau Claire company built its mill on the Bow River right in Calgary and within five years was the largest producer of lumber in the Northwest Territories. William H. Cushing's sash and door factory was the first in Alberta and from its establishment in 1884 steadily built a regional reputation for superior products. The presence of high-quality building stone around Calgary stimulated the growth of a local construction industry. Calgary stone was used to build the courthouse at Portage La Prairie and won a medallion at the Chicago World's Fair in 1896.[13] Stonemasons were the highest paid artisans in Calgary, earning up to $3.75 per day in the years of prosperity which accompanied the construction of the Calgary-to-Edmonton line. By securing favourable treatment from the civic authorities, Calgary's first manufacturers helped ensure their economic survival. By producing bulky, low-cost-per-dollar items, they were able to operate without competition from eastern Canadian or Winnipeg rivals.

Energetic boosters holding key positions in early local governments geared policies towards solidifying Calgary's economic base. Aspiring individuals whose vision and persuasiveness substituted for lack of personal success, these men included James Reilly and Wesley Fletcher Orr, who between them held the mayoralty five times in the 1890s. Reilly was a gregarious, self-styled ambassador in the classic booster tradition. The speaker's platform was his second home and he rarely missed an opportunity to dwell on the merits of Calgary or his own contributions. Orr was a far more complex figure. Frustrated but never disillusioned by earlier setbacks, Orr was totally committed to his

The Calgary Brewing and Malting Company was formed in 1892 by A.E. Cross (fourth from right). Cross had come to Alberta from the East in 1884 and soon became one of Calgary's most prominent citizens. At various times, he served as an M.L.A., president of the Board of Trade and president of the General Hospital.

adopted city. He was one of the original speculators who bought section 14 in 1883, and he gravitated towards local government in order to influence policies favourable to east Calgary. Over the years, Orr's interests in self-aggrandizement blurred easily into general boosterism, and Calgary never had a more ardent champion than this lonely, somewhat introspective figure who wrote thousands of letters promoting Calgary and its district.

Neither Reilly nor Orr was unique. There were enough others to make Calgary's local governments before 1900 agents of town promotion. Through annual amendments to the ordinance of the Northwest Territories that governed municipalities, the boosters on council increased decision-making powers at the local level. The policies of Calgary's civic governments reflected the strong influence of dominant booster-businessmen. Leading boosters used their positions to further their own interests and made little effort to conceal their ambitions. For example, Wesley Orr, after unsuccessfully working to delay incorporation, made no apologies for his strenuous promotion of east Calgary in council, even though it was common knowledge that he stood to profit extensively from settlement in the area. William Pearce was another who used his official position to enhance his own interests. Senator James A. Lougheed wielded political influence to secure favourable treatment for certain business enterprises in which he was involved. Certainly, the close-knit nature of this group enabled it to reconcile town promotion with personal profit.

An excellent example of promotion/profit was the industry bonussing policy adopted by council in 1888 on a motion put forward by Orr. As a result of this motion, the local authorities sought from the Legislative Assembly of the Northwest Territories the power to offer inducements to encourage industrial location in Calgary. This policy established generous tax exemptions, free building sites and bonuses to individuals manufacturing virtually any product. A locally made cigar, the Alberta Special, made its inconspicuous appearance around 1900. In spite of the absence of tanning bark, council whole-heartedly backed the establishment of a tannery in 1892. Within two years the owner was broke, even though committees of council had reported favourably on the healthy state of the operation. But by reducing operating costs, this booster policy did stimulate the growth of at least three of the city's more successful enterprises.

The company which manufactured Royal Crown soap, a big seller in later years, was bolstered by generous grants in the early 1890s. William H. Cushing's sash and door factory received special tax exemptions, and A. E. Cross and partners were reluctant to begin brewery operations until they received special considerations from council.

Council energetically promoted settlement and agriculture in and around Calgary, which one observer described as "new, rough, unhappy looking, but decidedly prosperous".[14] An immigration committee was formed in 1889, with its duties clearly outlined:

> . . . to answer all communications relating to the advantages and capabilities of the country for agricultural and stock purposes, to meet as far as possible all incoming settlers and to assist them in locating in this district and to advise them in matters relating to settlement, to circulate printed matter relating to the inducements offered by the surrounding country as may be procurable and to propound and submit to the full board such schemes as they may deem fit and necessary for the furtherance of settlement and the interests of the town.[15]

The result was a regular dispatch of promotional pamphlets to eastern Canada, the United Kingdom and the United States; deployment of local men as paid immigration agents; promotion of lectures by visiting agriculturists; and extravagant feting of visiting immigration delegations, especially the British, who were believed to make the best citizens. Council, which made substantial monetary contributions to the local Agricultural Society, was also instrumental in having James Reilly commissioned by the federal government to make a study of dairy farming in Iowa and its applicability to Alberta.

Neither expense nor imagination was spared by local boosters to promote town and district. In 1895, council was prepared to commit $25,000 towards the Territorial Fair if its venue were changed from Regina to Calgary. Official delegations rushed off to meet immigrant groups as far east as Port Arthur, only to discover that these people were already bound elsewhere. Considerable lobbying was conducted on various political levels to

Interior of Burns' meat-packing plant in the early 1900s. A daring businessman, Pat Burns became Calgary's first millionaire.

increase British government interest in the establishment of a remount for cavalry horses in the Calgary area.[16]

The efforts of council to secure the Imperial Remount and a Dominion Experimental Farm indicated the importance of permanent institutions to district development. The relationship between institutions and general economic growth was best illustrated in 1895, when the Dominion government set out to establish a sanatorium for consumptives. Council stated that "the location at Calgary of such an institute would be the initial of the introduction of more capital and the cause of more rapid development than any other source within our reach...."[17] Frequent meetings were held and petitions forwarded to leading political figures. A pamphlet entitled "Calgary, the Denver of Canada" was produced by the local committee promoting the sanatorium and was a classic example of the booster approach.[18]

Other individuals and organizations joined the town council in working to bring settlement and prosperity to the Alberta district. After Richard Hardisty's death in 1888, James A. Lougheed was named to the Canadian Senate. Lougheed possessed substantial land holdings and was involved in diverse commercial endeavours in Calgary. He was very active in local affairs and used his influence in Ottawa to encourage business investment in Calgary. He also guarded legislation favourable to local interests, such as water power rights on the Bow River.

One of the most dominant figures in Calgary during this period was William Pearce, Dominion superintendent of lands and mines.[19] Pearce's reputation as "the Czar of the West" was indicative of the influence he wielded with both the Conservative government and the CPR. He held substantial interests throughout Calgary and his residence in east Calgary was one of the finest west of Winnipeg. Nicknamed "Bow Bend Shack", this mansion was surrounded by trees and shrubs which advertised Pearce's keen interest in conservation and irrigation. In fact, Pearce was the driving force behind the movement to bring irrigation to southern Alberta. He worked with city council, the Board of Trade and the locally organized Irrigation League to mobilize public opinion and exert pressure on the federal government.[20] When the Northwest Irrigation Act was passed in 1894, the Calgary Irrigation Company, headed by William Pearce, was the first organization to take advantage of the new legislation. Among the original customers was the City of Calgary.

Railway promotion was a major means of attracting settlement and capital to the West. One town councillor remarked in 1888 that he "could draw up a petition praying the Angel Gabriel to come down and build a railway to the moon and get hundreds of signatures to it in Calgary".[21] Five railway charters were obtained by local interests before 1895. Two of these projected lines were to tap potential coal-producing areas, sources of power for industrial development. The federal government's reluctance to make land grants available in the 1890s doomed these ambitious schemes to failure. But the creation of the province of Alberta in 1905 and the encouragement given by the Liberal government to a second transcontinental line led to a revival of enthusiasm. The Calgary boosters were soon projecting 10 lines out of the city, one of which was to go to the Arctic Ocean.

It is difficult to assess the real impact of boosters in advertising the merits of Calgary and district. If success is measured in terms of practical results, then much of the promotional energy was in vain. Settlers did not flood into the area, nor did local voices hold much sway in most decisions effected by either the government or the CPR. The booster mentality symbolized a commercial aggressiveness nurtured mainly by an unshaken belief in the economic future of the West. These individuals were willing to work together in the general interest, and in many cases local rivalries were temporarily put aside. They were prepared to marshal the limited resources of local government behind a variety of promotional ventures which also involved a commitment of their own time. The diverse attempts by individuals and organizations to promote town and regional development indicated a dynamism and urban function that belied Calgary's small size.

POPULATION GROWTH AND ETHNIC RELATIONSHIPS

Calgary's small population during this period was fairly homogeneous in terms of ethnic origin and occupational base (Appendix, Tables III, IV, VII). Anglo-Saxons were dominant, and only the Chinese and people of native ancestry constituted sizeable ethnic minorities. Calgary's labour force, although containing a good number of self-employed, was oriented towards

Although they numbered only 63 in 1901, the Chinese were the largest non-Anglo-Saxon ethnic group in the city's early years. Many, such as Lee Bang, shown here in 1893, were employed as low-paid domestic servants to wealthy Calgarians.

skilled and semi-skilled categories. Few industries offered permanent employment to unskilled and transient labourers. Financial poverty and high unemployment were common.

Calgary's first two farmers and permanent residents, Sam Livingstone and John Glenn, were both Irishmen, and the small population which comprised Calgary before 1905 was almost entirely of British origin. Immigration figures for Calgary indicate that Anglo-Saxons outnumbered Europeans by a ratio of about seven to one in the early 1890s. The voters lists for Calgary in 1894-95 show columns of British names almost uninterrupted by names of obvious European origin.[22] Most of Calgary's business and social leaders were born in eastern Canada. Of these, a good percentage were from Ontario. Some, like William Roper Hull, George Clift King and Thomas Underwood, were English. Almost all were Protestant, with the Calgary district boasting the highest proportion of Anglicans in the Northwest Territories (Appendix, Table VIII).

The presence of the North West Mounted Police and the cattle industry strongly influenced the Anglo-Saxon tradition not only in Calgary but throughout southern Alberta. Many members of the NWMP were well-educated Britons who, according to one writer, were turned by the force into "magnificent material for a young country".[23] Some policemen, like George Clift King, Simon John Clarke and James Walker, later took up residence in Calgary. The NWMP, with its coterie of military officers, provided a symbol of the British aristocracy in an area where a growing ranching community adhered closely to the values of the British landed gentry. Calgary, as an urban extension of ranching interests, reflected this image. The Ranchmen's Club, formed in 1893, was the first selective institution of its kind in Calgary. Local polo and cricket teams epitomized the sporting pursuits of the privileged and often included ranchers and their sons. Members of the Calgary Hunt Club chased the hapless coyote across the Sarcee Indian Reserve. These hunts were formal affairs, including riders dressed in correct hunting outfits and a spectators' marquee.

Probably nowhere else in western Canada was the fusion of town and country elite as observable as it was around Calgary in the last decade of the nineteenth century. The Albertan ranching community tried to represent the standards of an established landed gentry in a frontier society. The large leaseholdings guarded Calgary like sentinels; there was little room for foreigners. As ranchers with their capital gravitated to Calgary and many local businessmen, including George Murdoch and Simon John Clarke, acquired property and became ranchers on a modified scale, ties between the elite of town and country were further strengthened.

During this period, Calgary's labour force reflected the city's marked orientation towards trade and commerce. It appeared as if most individuals who did not have their own businesses were employed as skilled artisans or clerks. Only three classes of artisans were reported by immigration officials in 1885. By 1891, 23 categories were listed. The presence of stone quarries and saw mills created a steady demand for masons and carpenters, who were the highest paid craftsmen throughout this period. Permanent work for unskilled labourers remained scarce, and consequently there was plenty of manpower available when the city began sewerage construction in 1890. Few establishments employed large numbers of people, and even then the work was seasonal. According to the 1891 Canadian census, Calgary's 600-man work force was employed in 146 commercial establishments.

As the population grew after 1900, there was a widening of the occupational base and the beginnings of an identifiable labour class. The Calgary Trades and Labour Council was formed in 1901 with three affiliated unions.[24] Two years later the first labour journal, the *Bond of Brotherhood*, made its appearance in the city. The Marxist rhetoric which punctuated this publication announced the presence of the class war in Calgary. The *Bond of Brotherhood* also kept local workers in touch with organizational activities in Calgary and informed them of developments on the international labour scene. The need for workers to live near their places of employment resulted in the emergence of loosely identified residential districts. Increasingly, small unserviced dwellings began to appear in proximity to the brewery and meatworks.

At the other end of the socio-economic scale, a relatively prosperous group provided commercial and social leadership. Many of these individuals shared unpleasant and routine tasks with their employees, and though some exhibited exclusiveness through handsome residences or winter holidays, they were at

Omuxapop Okrista, an elderly Sarcee woman.

For centuries prior to the arrival of white people in the Calgary region, the native people had maintained a proud and vital culture. This way of life was nearly destroyed by the intrusion of Anglo-Saxon settlement into southern Alberta. This Sarcee encampment, c. 1890, shows the growing town of Calgary in the background.

Women of the Blood tribe with dog travois. In the background, one of Calgary's first automobiles provides a vivid contrast in styles of transportation.

one with the rest of the population in enduring muddy streets, no sidewalks and summer stenches. Although servants were common, the shortage of reliable and capable domestic labour led to an informal employer-employee relationship. Calgary's business leaders were usually too busy to cultivate a lifestyle markedly different from that of their employees. Thus, social leadership generally came from churchmen, senior government officials and members of the professions. However, some individuals, like James A. Lougheed, Thomas Underwood and William H. Cushing, were prominent in both business and social reform.

Frontier Calgary's population was essentially transient. Many early residents were prospective farmers and ranchers who, for various reasons, had made Calgary their temporary home. Others were drifters who constituted a drain on the city's meagre welfare resources in the difficult years of the mid 1890s. A surprising number of businessmen left Calgary to seek better opportunities on the West Coast, in the United States or in the Klondike. Still others were victims of seasonal unemployment on the ranches and farms, in the saw mills and railway construction or in the construction industry in Calgary. Especially in the summer months, Calgary's population was swollen by young adults, many of them women, who moved in from surrounding settlements seeking employment.

This population movement resulted in a steady demand for permanent employment and the continuing presence of financial poverty. Permanent positions with the city were very popular, and in 1892 there were 46 applications for the one advertised teaching position.[25] In these years, bartering, begging and private debt holding were common. Some paid their rent by offering laundry services to their landlords, while others became dependent on the benevolence of private institutions to provide the necessities of life. In winter months, the immigration hall was sometimes used as a refuge. Coal thievery was prevalent, and many unemployed sought the haven and scanty rations available in the unsanitary municipal jail.

The widening of the socio-economic brackets had political implications. Elected municipal positions were denied to those who could not meet the high property qualifications. The result was the concentration of political power in the hands of the business and professional classes. The City Charter of 1893 provides an excellent example of a conscious policy pursued by large property holders to protect their interests. This charter, recommended by a special committee of the heaviest ratepayers, specified the unwarranted adoption of the ward system and the plural vote. In 1894, five per cent of the taxpayers cast about 33 per cent of the popular vote. Property qualifications for mayor and aldermen were raised to a level which disqualified over 60 per cent of the taxpayers from holding office. The *Bond of Brotherhood* proclaimed as one of its chief aims the lowering of the property qualification so that working men could run for civic office.[26]

By 1905, Calgary's population numbered approximately 10,000. It was predominantly Anglo-Saxon and young. At the turn of the century, children accounted for over 20 per cent of the population. Public apathy, high property qualifications and a substantial non-resident population enabled business and professional groups to control local politics. By 1905, this domination was still unchallenged. There were indications, however, that differentiation between segments of the population was becoming more definite. Clearly marked residential districts were beginning to emerge, and workers were becoming more conscious of their distinct identity.

During this period of overwhelming British and eastern Canadian influence, the Chinese were the most numerous non-Anglo-Saxon group in Calgary. The completion of the CPR meant unemployment for the many Chinese who had toiled mainly on the British Columbia stretch of the railroad. The first of these people filtered into Calgary in 1885-86 and they provided laundry services to the predominantly male population (Appendix, Table II). Because of restrictive immigration laws favouring the rich, the Chinese population grew slowly until, by 1901, they totalled 63. The first Chinese woman did not arrive in Calgary until 1889, and in the Dominion census of 1911 only three women were listed. For many years, long after later immigrant groups were well established, the Chinese population in Calgary could count few native-born Calgarians among their number.

Through discrimination or circumstance, the Chinese were willing to work long hours to perform necessary but menial services cheaply and efficiently. One strongly anti-Chinese resident of Calgary remarked in 1892 that "we can hardly get on

A studio portrait typical of the day features two Sarcees, Mutsenamakan and Stumetsekini.

A 205. MUTSENAMAKAN & STUMETSEKINI.
B. 866   SARCEE INDIANS.

Despite the racist attitudes of the dominant Anglo-Saxon majority, some native people did live in Calgary. Jim Big Plume and his wife and child are shown in front of their home in the 1890s.

The conversion of the native people to Christianity was a concern of most denominations active in the Calgary area. These Sarcee girls attended the Anglican mission in the 1890s.

without them".[27] These people were quick to adapt to their new surroundings and were able to work in an atmosphere of condescension. They became cooks and servants to the town and country moneyed class of the 1890s and soon began to specialize in restaurant and retail businesses. The laundry business in Calgary was virtually a Chinese monopoly.

After 1901, the Chinese congregated around their own businesses, which sprang up along Tenth Avenue near First Street West. Commercial activity had not spread extensively into this area, and it was here that land prices had shown their sharpest decline in the 1890s.[28] The Chinese were aided in their efforts to build a small community by Thomas Underwood. By allowing the Chinese to build on his land, Underwood was the first prominent businessman to support the Chinese community. Underwood's prestige as head of the Diamond Coal Company as well as his position as mayor in 1902-03 made him a valuable ally. For the most part, however, the Chinese were victims of overt racism and tolerated only because of their usefulness.

Ugly incidents associated with an outbreak of smallpox in 1892 revealed the hostility of the Anglo-Saxon majority. In July 1892, after smallpox was discovered in a laundry, a public outcry was directed against the supposedly unsanitary living conditions of the Chinese.[29] After the deaths of two non-Chinese, an outraged *Calgary Herald* termed the Chinese "an obnoxious element" and recommended their expulsion from the city.[30] Irate citizens threatened the Mounted Police with violence if they interfered with this necessary action. After a cricket match on August 3, a drunken mob attempted to terrorize the Chinese neighbourhood but was easily dispersed by the police, who had not taken the matter lightly. The NWMP superintendent noted in his report that two mounted sections had been kept ready for any emergency, "comprised of old cavalrymen who know how to use a sword".[31] The police quarantine and the efforts of the local medical authorities proved effective. The death toll was kept to four, and by the second week of August the scare was over.

Not all Calgary's leading citizens performed as capably as the Mounted Police, the doctors or the ministers who shielded the Chinese from danger. Police Chief Tom English not only failed to lend his support to the Mounted Police, but actually violated the quarantine by assaulting a guard who tried to prevent him from visiting one of his interned lady friends. Wesley Orr, probably the most influential member of the town council, was strongly anti-Chinese and during the controversy offered a free building site for a laundry run by whites to "assist in the philanthropic move of providing work to industrious and worthy whites and to make the presence of Mongolians in our midst totally unnecessary".[32] Mayor Alexander Lucas minimized the seriousness of the situation and presented accounts contradictory to those of the Mounted Police, who censured Lucas for his lack of leadership. Both Lucas and English were conveniently out of town at the height of unrest.

Native people occupied a lower position on the social scale than the Chinese and constituted Calgary's only other sizeable minority group during this period. They had gathered around Calgary since the fort days of the 1870s, and it was not uncommon in the 1880s to find a hundred tepees camped on the outskirts of town. Although there were some like George Murdoch who accepted the native people, the frequent bigoted allusions to them in the press indicated that they, perhaps even more than the Chinese, were victims of racism.[33] Yet like the Chinese, native people were exploited as a year-round source of cheap, menial labour. In fact, the Sarcees were virtually the only suppliers of firewood to Calgary in the 1880s. It was suggested in 1885 that the native people would pose no problems if local whites did not hire them to do odd jobs, but the real causes of the "problem" were rarely discussed.[34]

The prostitution of native women was, however, an undeniable fact of frontier life. The tragic Rosalie case in 1889, when a native girl was savagely murdered and mutilated by a white man, revealed that frontier justice in Calgary did not apply to native people. At the trial, the jury returned a verdict of "not guilty" in the face of overwhelming evidence to the contrary. Judge Charles B. Rouleau refused to accept the verdict and sent the chastised jury back to deliberate again. Upon its refusal, or inability, to reach a decision, the jury was dismissed and Rouleau ordered a new trial. After much difficulty, a jury was selected which found the defendant guilty of manslaughter.[35]

THE URBAN LANDSCAPE

Although Calgary's physical growth during this period was

contained within the corporate boundaries fixed in 1884, basic land-use patterns were clearly established by 1905. The site of the city, the presence of the CPR and individual decisions determined this process. The Calgary townsite was laid out west of the Elbow and south of the Bow Rivers on a triangle of relatively flat land. Immediately north of the Bow and directly opposite the townsite rose a 500-foot ridge which opened onto undulating prairie. The area to the east was interrupted by the Elbow River and the south-swinging Bow. The flat land upon which the town was built was broken by ravines and ridges to the south and west less than two miles from the railway station. This configuration of ridges, ravines and rivers effectively barred physical expansion by complicating the extension of utilities and requiring grades prohibitive to horse-drawn vehicles. Since access routes involved expensive bridge construction, it was not surprising to find underuse of areas separated by the rivers from the business centre.

The CPR mainline from Medicine Hat approached Calgary from the southeast and made a sharp swing to the west near the fort, bisecting the townsite as it followed the Bow River towards the Rockies. For reasons of its own, the CPR placed its station north of the tracks. The railway company probably envisaged a neat little town trending towards the Bow and stringing easterly to the fort and the original settlement. In any case, the proximity of the rails to the river effectively isolated the business community and produced discordant patterns of commercial development (see Map 2).

The most contentious issue of physical growth during this period concerned the direction of town expansion. Actually a continuation of the townsite debate, the controversy featured rival business interests determined to increase the value of their landholdings by encouraging commercial activity. The emergence of a manufacturing area in east Calgary and the association of this area with industrial land usage were important factors in Calgary's development. The convergence of railways was only part of the reason for the trend, which had been observable before the railway construction to either Edmonton or Fort Macleod. In the 1880s, east Calgary landholders, fearful of the western movement of the business centre, encouraged industries to locate on their properties outside the corporate limits.[36] The stockyards, abattoirs and brewery provided the nucleus, and by

1905 the pattern of manufacturing in east Calgary was established.

Three individuals were crucial in this development. All had extensive landholdings in east Calgary and all were powerful forces in their own right. William Pearce, James Walker and Wesley Orr wielded considerable influence on all political levels and in local business circles. In 1890, they almost persuaded the company building the railroad to Edmonton to locate its station in east Calgary.[37] Their aim was a rival town east of the Elbow. During these negotiations, Orr was still a member of town council. While Orr introduced the industry bonussing policy in council in 1888, it was Walker who recommended, in 1886, that the town purchase a quarter of section 11 in east Calgary so that the CPR could locate its stockyards there.[38] Within a short period, most of the rest of this crucial section was in the hands of these three major landholders.

The location of the stockyards in east Calgary was a pragmatic move. Section 11 was designated school land by the federal government, and therefore was neither open to normal homestead entry nor under the control of the CPR. Walker's suggestion that part of this section be acquired for stockyards and related purposes was accepted by both the town authorities and the CPR, who had not been able to agree on a suitable location. It was only after the stockyards were placed in east Calgary that Orr, Walker, Pearce and the town council initiated policies to entice further industrial activity on Section 11.

Although a nucleus of manufacturing was established in east Calgary during this period, other related enterprises were scattered on the north and south edges of the business centre. W. H. Cushing's sash and door factory was originally located on First Street West. The presence of the Eau Claire Lumber Mill on the south bank of the Bow River, almost adjacent to the business area, had a marked impact on subsequent land development patterns in the area. Other small manufacturing enterprises located nearby, with the result that the area between the river and the business centre became associated with manufacturing. By allowing the Eau Claire Company substantial rights in 1886, the town council temporarily relinquished its right to direct development along the south bank of the Bow River. By 1905, this attitude of civic indifference was reinforced by periodic floods, log jams

This view of Calgary, c. 1889, looks north from the Bow River. Although the population was still under 4,000, the landscape was beginning to assume the characteristics of an urban community.

OPPOSITE PAGE: *Calgary, c. 1885.*

and the tendency of nearby residents to use the south bank of the Bow River as a dumping ground for refuse. In their efforts to attract manufacturers to their properties, east Calgary landholders contributed to the subsequent abuse of natural beauty in the area encompassed by the bend in the Bow River as it swings south. Although William Pearce was responsible for major beautification projects on his own property, it was the presence of the Eau Claire Lumber Mill in downtown Calgary and council policies encouraging industry in east Calgary which resulted, by 1905, in inappropriate notions of land use along the south bank of the Bow River. Unfortunately, these attitudes were to prevail.

The CPR was a major factor in defining the extent of early Calgary's business district. By placing the railway station north of the tracks and by withdrawing lands immediately to the south from sale at the first auction of townsite lots, the CPR provided for a business district between the rails and the river. This commercial area concentrated itself around the railway station and extended two or three blocks towards the fort and the original settlement. The railway company gave its approval to this slightly eastward thrust of the business district by donating land in that area for civic purposes. Access to the south was across bumpy level crossings also chosen arbitrarily by the railway company. The distinct differentiation of commercial activity north and south of the tracks was further consolidated by the emergence of wholesale facilities south of the line directly opposite the business centre. In 1898, city council donated $25,000 to the CPR in return for the erection of freight sheds. The railway's decision to build these facilities in the downtown area east of Centre Street virtually ensured the development of the south side of the tracks for wholesale purposes. The resulting band of warehouses and spur line trackage was an effective buffer to potential retail and related commercial activities.

The erection of freight sheds also provided an impetus to the westward movement of the commercial centre. In the early 1890s, men like James A. Lougheed and George Alexander had begun to erect commercial blocks west of Centre Street along Eighth Avenue.[39] Poor economic conditions and slow population growth in the mid 1890s inhibited these early efforts to move the focus of business activity westward, but the later presence of the freight sheds revitalized this trend. As warehouses cropped up

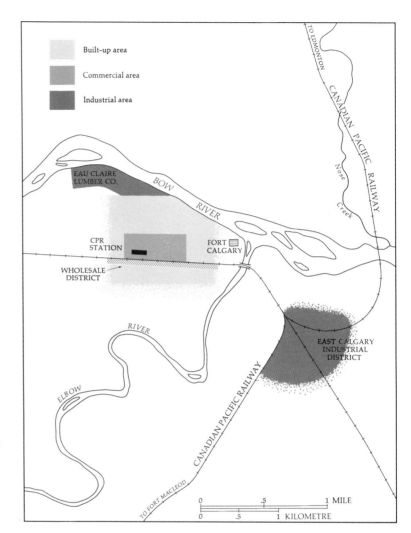

2 Calgary's Central Core, 1900

The Hudson's Bay Block, 1891. The Hudson's Bay Company has had stores in four locations in Calgary. This sandstone structure replaced a frame building on Eighth Avenue, east of the present Hudson's Bay location. Further additions were built in 1895 and 1905. In 1911, construction was begun on a larger store at the present site.

near the freight sheds, retail, professional and managerial establishments moved west along Ninth, Eighth and, to a lesser degree, Seventh Avenues. By 1905, Calgary's retail and business area was sandwiched between the Bow River on the north and the CPR mainlines to the south. Expansion east was limited by the freight yards and manufacturing activities beyond the Elbow River. The pattern for the probable westward movement of the business district was, in a sense, ordained before major population influx made its presence felt (see Map 3).

Calgary was very much a "walking city" during this period. Owners erected houses near their places of business. Accordingly, areas that could be loosely described as residential were along streets and avenues that adjoined the main commercial establishments. Houses of varying shapes and sizes were built. Some were large, handsome stone residences, while others were flimsy clapboard structures on 25-foot lots. Even tents were common during the summer months. Yet it could be argued that by 1905 some patterns of residential land use were discernible.

Fine houses were concentrated to the south along Twelfth and Thirteenth Avenues behind the developing wholesale district. Here, owners felt they could enjoy privacy and exclusiveness while remaining within easy walking distance of the business centre. Some of these residences were grand establishments. Erected on several lots and crafted by skilled European artisans, these mansions became the pride of Calgary and were exhibited freely in local promotional publications. James A. Lougheed's home "Beaulieu", erected in 1889, was among the most elaborate. The *Herald* published weekly reports on its progress during construction. Pat Burns built his sandstone residence nearby at the turn of the century. This castle-like structure contained ten bedrooms and four bathrooms and rooms finished in quarter oak with solid oak doors. Impressive buildings throughout this area made it Calgary's first exclusive neighbourhood.

It was during this period that boosters began referring to Calgary as "the Sandstone City". Beginning in 1887 with the construction of Knox Presbyterian Church, the presence of several handsome sandstone buildings gave Calgary a distinctive appearance. Some, like the courthouse (1888) and the Alberta Hotel (1888), were of plain design, while others, like the Alexander Corner (1891) or Pat Burns' mansion, were far more elaborate

and showed the architectural eclecticism that was to become a recurring feature in Calgary's stone buildings.

Difficulty of access made expansion north of the Bow neither feasible nor desirable. Although the view from the top of the ridge was Calgary's finest, there were few who braved the precipitous incline observable in early photographs of the north hill. However, it was land use north of the Bow during this period that dashed any hopes of eventually developing the north hill into an exclusive residential area. Following the completion of the Bow Marsh and Langevin bridges across the Bow River, small settlements established themselves on the narrow flats below the ridge. Most dwellings were unserviced and erected by owners who wished to avoid paying taxes. The presence of "shack towns" outside the corporate limits of urban centres was a fairly common phenomenon in western Canada. Early in the twentieth century, Calgary's German population congregated at Bridgeland near the Langevin Bridge. Farther east were the brothels of the Nose Creek area and a few primitive meatworks. By the time the north hill was taken into the city limits in 1907 and 1910, its second-class reputation was already established. By 1905, it was clear that areas of desirable residential growth would be to the south and southwest of the business centre. After 1900, land prices were rising fastest in that portion of the city. With the upsurge in the real estate market around 1904, the gradual movement towards the southwest was underway.

THE URBAN COMMUNITY: SOCIAL AND POLITICAL LIFE

Local government was the preserve of businessmen during this period, particularly after Calgary was incorporated as the first city in the Northwest Territories in 1893. The Citizens' Committee struck to examine the proposed city charter read like a "Who's Who?" of the local business community. Under the charter, property qualifications for positions of mayor and councillors were raised considerably in favour of the business community. In 1887, the average assessment of members of council was over $10,000 compared to a town average of approximately $900. Since they contributed the bulk of the taxation revenue, merchants generally felt that the responsibility of government was theirs by right. Certainly Senator James A. Lougheed inferred as much in

Boosters often referred to Calgary as ''Sandstone City''. This view of Eighth Avenue in 1892 suggests why the term was used. Stone quarries in the area provided Calgary with sturdy grey sandstone, which gave the local architecture a successful and confident appearance.

COPYRIGHT
ERNEST BROWN.

542 THE ALBERTA HOTEL, CALGARY. 1891.

The Alberta Hotel, 1891. This impressive building was constructed in 1888-89 and became the city's most celebrated "watering hole". Located on the southeast corner of Eighth Avenue and First Street West, the Alberta Hotel survived as a commercial block after Prohibition in 1916.

OPPOSITE PAGE: *The bar of the Alberta Hotel was known as the longest bar in Alberta. In the 1950s, Picardy's store occupied this location.*

1889 when he maintained that large ratepayers should receive preferential treatment.[40]

In that year, civic elections were suspended and a mayor and council chosen by the business community. Their rationale, as expressed by one observer, was simple:

> . . . to do justice to themselves [the businessmen] and to the town of Calgary it was necessary to place at the head of affairs a man of thorough business training and sound judgement. . . . Following this consent the feeling became prevalent that a council chosen from the businessmen of the town be considered.[41]

It is therefore not surprising that almost all members of the town and city councils during these years were merchants. Some early mayors, like Daniel Webster Marsh (1889), Dr. James Lafferty (1890), William H. Cushing (1900) and Thomas Underwood (1902-1903), were leaders in the business community. Usually, the more aggressive of these elected officials headed up crucial standing committees such as finance or public works. The chairmen of these committees, depending on their political acumen and energy, could appropriate funds and effect decisions quite arbitrarily. Wesley Orr used his perennial position as chairman of the public works committee between 1889-96 to pursue policies favourable to east Calgary.

Spending priorities of municipal government in Calgary before 1900 attest to the dominance of businessmen in local politics. Money was difficult to raise in these years, particularly given the CPR's refusal to pay municipal taxes on its extensive landholdings within the town limits.[42] Although this matter was finally settled in 1889-90 on a proportional basis, Calgary's small population carried a heavy tax burden during these years. With borrowing power limited by statute, civic officials were obliged to exercise considerable discrimination in budgetary matters. Attention was paid to road surfacing and sidewalk construction in the business area. Access roads to the retail district were kept in reasonably good repair. Councils ensured that utilities were extended first to the business section. Residential parts of the town were accorded priority in the installation of utilities on the basis of their proximity to the busy commercial core. Promotional publications were adequately funded. In 1890, council spent

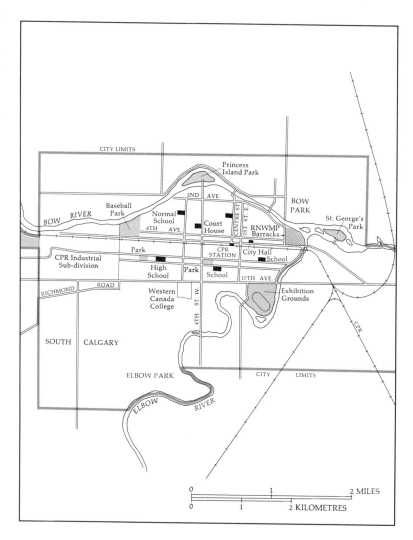

3 Calgary in 1908

Wesley Fletcher Orr

Sir James Lougheed

Thomas Underwood

William Pearce

$3,000 in an unsuccessful attempt to find natural gas within the town limits. Eight years later, the CPR received $25,000 in return for the freight yards.

Expenditures for social services received a much lower priority. In 1895, impetus for the first municipal hospital came not from council, but from the Women's Hospital Aid Society. Indeed, there had been considerable opposition in council to the idea of a general hospital, and in 1890 the members had tried to avoid responsibility for cemetery supervision and maintenance. Plans for financial assistance to fund a public library were also ignored in council.[43] Similarly, as noted by William Pearce in 1902, the civic authorities did little to honour their commitment to improve the islands in the Bow River donated by the federal government for recreational purposes:

> The islands in the Bow River which would add very much to the beauty of the place have been granted to the city 14 or 15 years ago on the distinct understanding that $100 per year should be spent in the way of improving them. The *total* outlay in this regard has not exceeded probably $100.[44]

In most cases involving expenditures for social services, councillors and aldermen maintained that responsibility for such services belonged to religious organizations, charitable societies or private enterprise.

Fiscal inadequacies and a strong faith in private enterprise led councils to endorse private ownership of utilities during this period. While there was some sentiment in council favouring municipal ownership of essential utilities, the city took possession only after private operations proved inadequate and, to a degree, expensive. Originally, the water supply came from public wells dug at various points in the town. Tracings of one of these wells were unearthed when excavating began for the construction of the present Hudson's Bay building. These public wells were supplemented by sunken tanks and water delivery wagons. In 1887, some local businessmen formed a company and petitioned council for the right to install a town waterworks. Eventually, members of the company were elected to council,[45] and when George Alexander proved able, in 1889, to raise the necessary capital in Britain, council gave its approval to a privately owned town waterworks. It even agreed to Alexander's stipulation that the town construct its own sewerage system in conjunction with the waterworks.

The venture was not successful. Relations between Alexander and council were often tense and sometimes openly antagonistic. Efficiency of service fell far short of expectations. The water supply from the Bow River was far from satisfactory. Matters came to a head in 1895 when William H. Cushing's factory caught fire and water pressure was inadequate to fight the blaze. Law suits followed and in 1900, with Cushing himself as mayor, the city purchased the antiquated waterworks for $90,000.[46] By this time, council was convinced that efficient service depended on municipal ownership.

Businessmen also dominated the companies which generated electric power. Monopolies, granted in early years to private companies, continued until a need for increased service forced the city into more direct control. The first company to generate electricity in 1887 was owned in part by Mayor George Clift King, D.W. Davis from Fort Macleod and Alberta's lone representative in the House of Commons, and E.B. Braithwaite, manager of the Bank of Montreal. However, this company could not compete with the Calgary Water Power Company, formed by Peter Prince of the Eau Claire Lumber Company in 1889. Prince utilized the water wheel at his mill on the Bow River to produce sufficient power to provide somewhat erratic service. Prince was backed by supporters on council as well as by Senator James A. Lougheed, who, in 1890, secured passage of a bill in Ottawa which favoured Prince's water power rights on the Bow River. In 1894, Prince received from council a 10-year monopoly to supply electricity to the city. In 1904, when Prince's monopoly came up for renewal, it was obvious that, particularly during the winter, the water wheel produced inefficient and inadequate service. When Prince proved recalcitrant, council looked favourably on the suggested solution of municipal ownership. The result was the construction of the city steam-generating plant in 1905.

In 1892, council began to explore the possible acquisition of corporate water power rights on the Elbow River. A bylaw was actually passed in 1894 to raise $35,000 for the establishment of an electric light plant by the corporation. If private companies were granted exclusive water power privileges, the city would lose the right to offer certain inducements to potential industries. Some

*Mrs. George Barclay
Bruce and daughters,
Christmas Day, 1893.*

Christmas Day 1893

Calgary Canada

Symphony orchestra in the early 1900s. Conductor J.J. Young is at centre, and Kathleen Parlow, world famous violinist, is in the front row, far left.

CAMROSE LUTHERAN COLLEGE
Library

Hull's Opera House, built by William Roper Hull in 1893. Hull was a prominent Calgarian, active in local business, stock raising and social life. He also built and owned the Calgary Grain Exchange Building, the Alberta Block, the Victoria Block and the Albion Block.

An interior view of Hull's Opera House, with a seating capacity of 1,000.

proponents of municipal ownership on council were mainly concerned with denying Prince his monopoly. To these individuals, municipal ownership was a political device to thwart a specific individual. During this period, there was little popular support or political conviction behind municipal ownership. Public control of water and electric utilities came more through practical necessity than conviction.

In general, there was little public interest in civic affairs in frontier Calgary. Most municipal elections were lacklustre events, regarded more for their betting potential than as expressions of popular will. Voting turn-outs were often embarrassingly low, despite efforts by the press and candidates to fire interest at the polls, and meetings called to discuss matters of immediate concern aroused little public enthusiasm. While the business community did dominate the civic political arena and pursued policies primarily designed to further the commercial growth of Calgary, it was certainly in the face of little opposition and general apathy.

Dependent on the CPR and the ranching industry — both creations, in a sense, of the federal Conservative Party—Calgary was strongly Conservative in federal politics from the outset. James Reilly once remarked that he and Dr. James Lafferty were the only Liberals south of the Bow River.[47] The local Conservative Association was a vigorous body which held senior members of the party, particularly Sir John A. Macdonald, in almost religious awe. However, adherence to federal Conservatism did little to help Calgary in the House of Commons before 1896 and definitely prejudiced its interests in the capital dispute of 1905.

Before 1903, Alberta was a single federal constituency. From 1887 to 1896, this seat was filled by D. W. Davis, a Conservative from Fort Macleod. Though Davis had vested interests in Calgary, he was hardly sensitive to the city's specific needs. Aside from being a spokesman for ranching interests, Davis made little impact in the House. One of his rare utterances in Parliament was to the effect that he was taking off his coat for a fight. Wesley Orr, also an ardent Conservative, referred to Davis as a "mere whisky trader". When the able, articulate Frank Oliver of the *Edmonton Bulletin* ran as a Liberal in 1896, Calgary, with the rest of Alberta, rejected Conservatism. This uncharacteristic swing to Liberalism was not to last in Calgary, which in 1900 unsuccessfully sup-

ported R. B. Bennett, James A. Lougheed's law partner, against Oliver. Three years later when Calgary received its first seat in the Commons, it promptly elected a Conservative and, therefore, found itself without a member on the government side of the House when the capital debate broke in 1905.

When the federal Liberal Party decided, in 1905, to form two provinces from the old Northwest Territories, Frank Oliver was a senior member of the government who had received a cabinet position when Clifford Sifton resigned. His preference for his home town of Edmonton was the telling point in the bitter capital dispute. Oliver was instrumental in having Edmonton named provisional capital until its status was ratified or changed by the first elected provincial government. Provincial constituencies were fixed arbitrarily in Ottawa under the direction of the Minister of the Interior, who happened to be Frank Oliver. In what seemed a blatant gerrymander to Calgarians, the electoral boundaries were drawn to give the northern half of the province a numerical advantage in the House unwarranted by population. Accordingly, Edmonton was later ratified as the permanent capital.

The loss of the capital was a bitter blow to Calgary. As the largest city in the Northwest Territories and the centre of the province's most prosperous region, Calgary felt its claims to be more legitimate than those of any other town. Calgary had led the drive for responsible government and provincial status. The Northwest League, formed in Calgary in 1886, proclaimed provincial status as one of its chief aims, while the Provincial Rights Association had a large membership in the city by the early 1890s.[48] James A. Lougheed and James Reilly were acknowledged as being two of the most informed men in the Territories on the subject of provincial autonomy. Hugh Cayley from Calgary was prominent in the Territorial Assembly during the movement towards responsible government. Frederick Haultain, generally regarded as the driving force and father of provincial status for Alberta and Saskatchewan, represented a southern Alberta constituency. Calgary had taken the lead in initiating changes in territorial legislation affecting municipalities. In the late 1880s, a local group attempted to have the capital of the Northwest Territories alternate between Regina and Calgary. Although the move was unsuccessful and Regina remained the sole capital, Calgary's

ON TENNIS MATCH, PLAYED AT CALGARY JANY 23RD 1892.   BOORNE & MAY, CALGARY, N.W.T.

Tennis in Calgary, January 1892. This court was located on the northeast corner of Fourth Avenue and Centre Street South. Calgary's steeply rising north hill is in the background.

Born in Ontario in 1846, James Walker came west in 1874. He joined the NWMP and served as inspector for seven years. A successful real estate man and active in local organizations such as the school board, hospital board and humane society, Colonel James Walker was named Calgary's "Citizen of the Century" in 1975. He is shown here in 1901 with his son Selby at his home in east Calgary.

Living quarters at the British American Ranch (once the Cochrane Ranch) west of Calgary, c. 1886. The man on the couch is Ernest B. Cochrane.

leadership role in Alberta was clearly emphasized. Yet despite the most strenuous and sustained efforts of its spokesmen, Calgary saw the capital, with all its economic and political advantages, go to the smaller, Liberal Edmonton.

There was a saying in Calgary that Calgary skies and Tory blue went together. During this period, it was as true of local politics as it was federally. Leaders of local government, the church and society were, with few exceptions, avowed Conservatives. Calgary's leading newspaper, the *Herald*, was the mouthpiece of Conservative ideals. There were a few members of the business community with Liberal affiliations, but some of these were classed as errant Conservatives rather than genuine Grits. However, despite early Calgary's general allegiance to Conservatism, group action on local issues would often transcend traditional political affiliations.[49] Both Conservatives and Liberals occupied executive positions concurrently on the Northwest League, formed in 1886 to agitate for favourable treatment for Calgary in the Territorial Assembly. The Provincial Rights Association also represented considerable majority opinion, and in an essay contest on the subject in 1895, the three judges included two strong Liberals and one Conservative. The Irrigation League featured a similar cross section of political opinion.

Calgary's social growth during this period was closely linked to the birth and development of institutions. Limitations imposed by the frontier played a large part in the selection and early growth of these institutions. The most viable were those subject to centralized control; those relying on local authority were less stable. And so, the formalization of local institutions during the first decade of the twentieth century marked Calgary's passage through one stage of frontier influence.

The financial barrenness that characterized early Calgary had its effects on social organizations. Before 1891, the Board of Trade could not maintain itself, and up to 1900 it was virtually an extension of the civic government. Musical bands provided a major source of entertainment in early Calgary, yet they flourished only under the auspices of larger bodies, such as the North West Mounted Police. A town band did not become feasible until 1889, when the fire department assumed its organization and Daniel W. Marsh donated instruments. Despite efforts by influential figures such as Bishop Cyprian Pinkham as early as

1890, private schools could not survive in Calgary before the early 1900s, and then they catered to small enrolments.[50]

Within a decade of incorporation, a few wealthier residents had formed numerous private societies in the city and these generally needed little financial support to survive. The Calgary Turf Club revealed the local interest in horses, and the Calgary Operatic Society produced its first operetta, "The Pirates of Penzance", in 1895. Most societies were organized along formal lines, usually copying the constitutions and practices of established models in eastern Canada. The Ranchmen's Club was modelled on the St. James Club in Montreal. Literary, scientific, historical, dramatic and musical societies joined bicycle, hockey, shooting, hunt, curling, cricket and lacrosse clubs to provide ample recreational pursuits. Visiting lecturers and troupes of entertainers were assured receptive audiences in the Hull Opera House, built by William Roper Hull on the corner of Sixth Avenue and Centre Street.

The church was a cohesive force in early Calgary. Aside from the very obvious force of moral authority, the church also provided the centralized structure and financial security necessary for survival and development in a frontier environment. All major denominations enjoyed marked success in this period.[51] The Methodist church could afford to pay its minister an annual salary of $1,000 in 1887. A weekly parade of Mounted Police, often accompanied by their marching band, attended the Anglican church. Family pews in the Anglican church indicated social status. The William Pearce family held a prominent place, and Pearce himself was outspoken on issues relating to the church. Most leading citizens were good church attenders, and some were particularly active in church work. William H. Cushing taught Sunday school. John J. Young of the *Herald* was organist and choirmaster for Central Methodist Church, and William Davidson, owner of the *Albertan*, was the son-in-law of a Presbyterian grand superintendent. Pat Burns was probably the best known Catholic in western Canada. Prosperous parishioners were generally directors of the various church bodies and guaranteed the loans for church building programs. The influence of the frontier was such that the church in early Calgary filled a role disproportionate to that in older established centres. Civic authorities showed little concern for social matters, and so

Hunters and dogs at the Rawlinson Brothers' Ranch west of Calgary in the early 1900s. Many of Calgary's Anglo-Saxons attempted to recreate the lifestyle they had known in England. Outdoor activities, including hunting, fishing, polo, cricket and picnicking, were popular.

the churches provided leadership in combatting social problems. Church relief agencies often catered to needy parishioners and impoverished immigrants.

The various masonic orders also flourished in early Calgary. In 1885, George Murdoch, in his written defence of his first year in office, referred to a prevailing opinion that the masons were running the town. By 1890, there were at least five masonic orders with long membership lists. With memberships based primarily on common ethnic backgrounds or religious affiliations, the masonic orders contributed to the social life of Calgary. They provided ceremonies at the opening of the town waterworks in 1890. The English lodges carried on a British tradition by holding annual paperchases and English dinners. A feature attraction in one year was a slide exhibition of the Sudan War.

At this time, however, the local educational system lacked the strong, centralized authority exhibited by the church and masonic orders. Both funding and public pressure were inadequate. The Northwest Territories Act had provided the administrative formula for the establishment of school districts, the standardization of curricula and teacher training, based on the Ontario model. But local control limited the entire process, and education in the first 20 years was hardly the positive force it was expected to be.[52]

The financial burden for education fell on the local taxpayer. In 1896, the school board's operating budget totalled a little over $13,000. More than $9,000 came from council grants. Penny-pinching councils curtailed expenditures, and well-qualified teachers were not attracted to Calgary. Five of the nine Calgary teachers in 1893 were without certification. James Short and his first assistant received their notices of termination from the board in 1892. Their salaries were considered too high ($1,200 and $1,000 per annum). Subsequent notices in Toronto advertised these positions at a 20 per cent lower salary. In 1895, council asked the board to effect further reductions. In the same year, the first assistant received the same salary as the town scavenger, or collector of night soil.

Local academic standards were not high. In 1890, 13 Calgary students wrote the territorial university entrance examination. None passed. Yet the overall proportion of passes in the Northwest Territories was over 60 per cent. It is understandable why those who could afford the expense sent their children to private schools in the East. In 1903, lack of confidence in the educational system was freely expressed at a large general meeting called to gauge public attitudes towards the problems facing education in the city.

School morale was often low during this period. There were many references to the unruly behaviour of Calgary students. Even Sunday school classes experienced discipline problems. However, given the cheerless nature of Calgary classrooms, the high enrolments and meagre equipment, it was not surprising to find poor discipline and low attendance. In 1892, one class had 88 students on its roster, but an average attendance of 27. Despite official reports to the contrary, the average daily attendance was not much over 50 per cent during these years.[53] School and community relations were not amicable. In a corporal punishment controversy in 1892, a group of parents conducted a "witch hunt" on various teachers. The well-attended public meetings were often bitter affairs, and it was apparent that there was not only a lack of confidence in the schools but also a lack of direction from either the board or the few underpaid teachers.

Local law enforcement in early Calgary was also a haphazard affair. To be sure, there were few crimes of violence involving death, and there were frequent allusions to Calgary's peaceable nature compared with frontier towns in the United States. But this law enforcement came from the NWMP, under whose strong centralizing authority much of the Canadian West was controlled. However, when the workings of justice devolved on local authorities, an immature stage of institutional development was quite evident. Calgary's small police force was under the direct control of council, particularly the mayor. Communication between the two was poorly defined and informal. Early police chiefs were rough individuals who often exercised questionable prerogatives to dispense instant justice. After his dismissal in 1887, the first police chief held rigged dice games and finally left town owing $3,000.[54] Tom English, chief from 1890 to 1909, was a rugged frontier lawman who ran the town effectively but with a cavalier disregard for rules or procedure. Policemen were poorly paid and enjoyed little job security. One constable who had his salary increased for honesty and diligence suffered demotion and later dismissal all under the auspices of the same council.

Inexpert justices of the peace and poorly framed bylaws contributed to a lack of respect for the law. George Murdoch revealed in his diary that he conducted each case on its individual merits. Two justices of the peace in the 1890s were accused of pocketing fines. Each tried the other's case, not so amicably it seems, for they began to fight in the courtroom. Another justice of the peace imposed a minimal fine on an individual who had resisted arrest in public view. Yet another claimed that many infractions went unpunished because of interference by sympathetic aldermen.[55] Given these lax practices, it was not suprising to find crowds hindering policemen making arrests or to hear leading citizens request that the Mounted Police take over law enforcement in town.

By 1905, Calgary's population was beginning to increase. Growing prosperity and greater borrowing powers were giving the city the financial muscle it needed to overhaul its educational and police systems. But Calgary was still a town of contrasts, with the influence of the frontier yielding slowly to more urban pressures. These were the halcyon days before population influx transformed the nature of the frontier and, with it, Calgary's self-image.

Chapter Two
Emerging City
1906-1914

With the closing of the American frontier, the Canadian plains came into their own as the "last best West". The Laurier government's intensive immigration campaign finally paid off in the years after 1900 as thousands of settlers from eastern Canada, Europe and the United States poured into the West. From 1901 to 1911, Alberta's population jumped from 72,000 to 375,000, and booster rhetoric seemed determined to keep pace:

> Men and women count for more here than they do in the East. To us is entrusted a domain greater than the empires of old.... Sincerity of religious life, sanctity of home and integrity of business conduct are all being established in Alberta.[1]

This boom period marked Calgary's birth as a regional city and determined conditions that affected subsequent urban expansion.

ECONOMIC GROWTH AND METROPOLITAN DEVELOPMENT

Agriculture prospered under favourable market conditions, improved seed strains and farming techniques and mechanization. Some 80,000 acres were under field crops in 1898. By 1910, the figure was 3.3 million acres. Yields were equally impressive. Oat production increased from 3.7 million bushels in 1900 to 17 million bushels in 1910. But most significant was the success of the wheat crops. From less than 800,000 bushels in 1900, the wheat yield in Alberta soared to over 9 million bushels in 1910. In the same year, the value of Alberta field crops was estimated at over $17 million, a figure that approximated the total value of cattle in the province.[2]

It was during these years that Calgary gained primacy as a regional wholesale and distributing centre. Rural population growth and the rise of smaller important urban centres like Red Deer, Wetaskiwin and Lethbridge increased the need for a central distributing point that could store and market the agricultural equipment and manufactured articles necessary to sustain a commercial rural economy. There were over 150 wholesale and jobbing houses in Calgary by 1911, while the CPR handled over 700 freight cars daily as early as 1907. Calgary became regional headquarters for agricultural implement dealers, commercial travellers and financial houses. Hotels and warehouses proliferated. High rental rates for retail spaces in Calgary meant that retailing suffered at the expense of wholesale activities. Local organizations like the Board of Trade and the municipal governments were well aware of the importance of the wholesale trade to Calgary and made strenuous efforts to gain freight rate preferences. Only a few years later, in the sober aftermath of the boom, Calgary's business leaders were to state unequivocally that the wholesale trade was all the city had to fall back on.[3]

Calgary's growth as a regional centre during these years was consolidated by railway construction. Local boosters were active in pressuring the provincial government to intensify its railway construction program after 1907. In 1908, the Board of Trade published a special report on railways in which it stated that railway construction "should be assisted by every man, woman and child in Calgary".[4] By 1914, the Canadian Northern and the Grand Trunk Pacific had built lines to the city, and Calgary's

The first Grand Trunk Pacific train, 1912. Although extensive passenger service was anticipated, the Grand Trunk never operated in Calgary as a paying line.

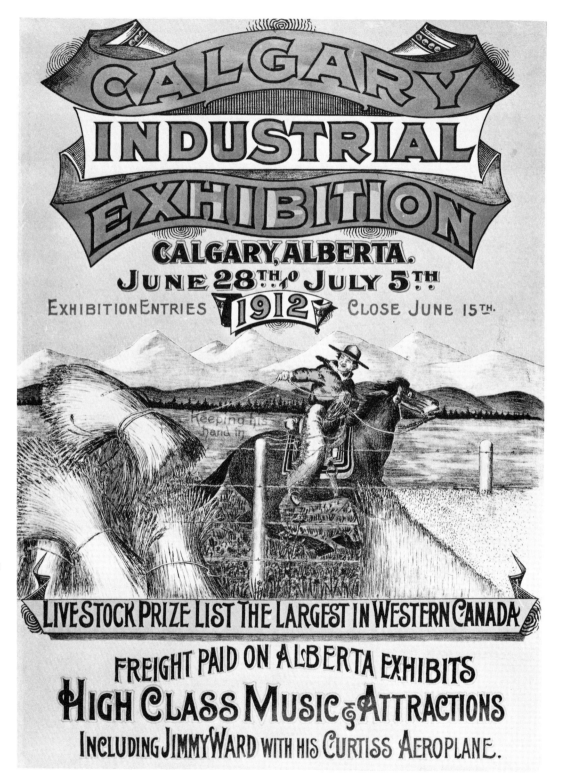

The Calgary Exhibition was in business for many years before the advent of the Stampede. Colonel James Walker arranged for a grant of land to be used for the Calgary Agricultural Exhibition in 1884. In 1900, the Calgary Agricultural Society was re-organized as the Inter-Western Pacific Exhibition Company and 11 years later became the Calgary Industrial Exhibition.

position in the western Canadian railway network was rivalling that of Winnipeg.

Calgary's status as a regional centre was enhanced in other ways. By 1911, the CPR had spent a total of $16 million on irrigation in southern Alberta and had created more than one million acres of arable land. Calgary became administrative headquarters for this enormous undertaking and the main distributing point for irrigation supplies. Calgary also became the headquarters of various provincial livestock associations and the site of annual sales and exhibitions. The 1908 Dominion Fair was the biggest event of its kind held in Calgary to that date.

The small manufacturing base established in the 1890s expanded to meet regional demands, and according to the 1911 census, Calgary counted 46 establishments employing 2,133 workers (Appendix, Table I). There was a continued emphasis on food processing and building materials, with a growing concentration on foundry products. One aspect of the expansion was the success of long-established concerns. Pat Burns marketed his White Carnation and Shamrock Leaf meat products in 61 retail outlets throughout Alberta, Saskatchewan and British Columbia. William H. Cushing, too, became rich. His 10-acre plant in east Calgary employed 200 workers and manufactured over 400 doors daily.[5] With factories in Edmonton, Regina and Saskatoon and branches at Red Deer and Fort Saskatchewan, Cushing made his XLCR brand a regional name. The Calgary Brewing and Malting Company employed a permanent staff of over 100, and owner A. E. Cross created his own market by buying hotels throughout Alberta and Saskatchewan. There was certainly good money to be made in the brewing business judging from some rather acerbic comments. The High River Times noted that at two glasses for 25 cents brewers were fast becoming millionaires.[6] Calgary journalist Bob Edwards, in his 1907 letter of resignation from the Board of Trade, was far more caustic when he observed that brewers flourished in Alberta because there was no bounty on wolves.

The small soapworks which almost went broke in 1892 changed hands in 1908 and soon after was turning out over 1,000 pounds of soap monthly, most of it the well-known Golden West Soap. In a province-wide promotional scheme, a company representative visited homes with envelopes containing certificates for purchase in various Calgary retail stores. Upon producing a Golden West soap label, the homeowner earned the right to choose one of these envelopes. The contest, endorsed and carried widely by the Herald, was immensely popular and did much to advertise a local product. The Eau Claire Lumber Company employed over 150 men and handled more than 50,000 feet of lumber per day. Crown Lumber Company, with headquarters in Calgary, operated 52 yards, making it the largest lumber concern in western Canada. The Calgary yard alone needed a trainload of materials every second day to meet requirements.[7]

Although total manufacturing in Calgary increased by approximately 1,500 per cent in the decade 1901-11, markets remained local and regional.[8] Few industries established clientele beyond the province. Similarly, Calgary offices of American, eastern Canadian or even Winnipeg-based companies had little autonomy. Decisions involving minor expenditures needed head office approval. So, while Calgary's importance was enhanced during these years of prosperity, the city's economic role was defined within limited, regional parameters. Calgary's failure to challenge Winnipeg as a grain centre and the flagging fortunes of the cattle industry clearly restricted the city's metropolitan development.

The Alberta wheat farmer benefited least from western Canada's surge to agricultural prosperity. Discriminatory freight rates lessened his return from wheat sales by approximately seven cents per bushel as compared with his counterparts in Manitoba.[9] Winnipeg was North America's leading grain centre, handling 88 million bushels in 1909. Calgary was not even Alberta's largest shipping point in that year.

Calgary's chief response to Winnipeg's domination of the grain trade lay in the promotion of the Pacific ports as terminals for Alberta wheat. Even before the Panama Canal was opened in 1914, it was held that the popular winter wheat, Alberta Red, could undersell spring wheat freighted through Fort William on the Liverpool market. The "big ditch", as the Panama Canal was called, would prove the point. Richard Bedford Bennett remarked on his return from a visit to Europe in 1909 that Calgary was regarded as the centre of the richest and most productive part of Canada and that much interest had been expressed in the experiment of shipping Alberta wheat to Liverpool via the

Calgary road construction crew, 1912.

The waterworks was one of Calgary's first municipally owned utilities. Opened in 1890 under private ownership, the town waterworks provided inadequate service and was purchased by the City of Calgary in 1900.

Quarrying stone for the CPR station. When the first train reached Calgary in 1883, a portable structure was erected on Fourth Street S.E. The next year, a boxcar without wheels served as a depot, and in 1893, a sandstone depot and dining room were constructed on Centre Street. When increasing rail traffic made a larger station necessary, the old building was dismantled, and work began on a new station in 1907. The CPR station opened in 1912 and served until 1968, when it was torn down to make way for Palliser Square.

Pacific.[10] Beginning in 1908, efforts were made to establish terminal elevators in Vancouver, hitherto regarded as "the granite block" in the way of the Pacific trade. In this respect, the formation of the Calgary Grain Exchange in 1909 represented a gesture of confidence. There were some indications of success. Trial shipments were begun, and the federal government built an elevator in Calgary at a cost of $1 million.[11] Other elevators were erected in the city designed primarily for western shipments. There were, however, factors militating against the Pacific route. The farmers' organizations were more interested in bettering their collective lot, and to them the Pacific route was secondary to more basic concerns. The CPR appeared so disinterested that it was alleged that the company actually opposed western wheat shipments.[12] Thus, during the bumper crop of 1915, the Calgary elevators stood idle, and on November 27 the *Herald* commented that the elevators "were born a little before their time".

As in earlier years, Calgary relied heavily on the livestock industry. Here there was no Winnipeg with which to contend, and the local boosters were always at their best describing the Alberta rangelands. Yet these were not good years for cattlemen. Beset by financial woes and doubts over the future of grazing in the West and concerned about the growing dominance of American beef-packing houses, many ranchers had left Alberta by 1912. With such uncertainty surrounding the future of the livestock industry, Calgary failed to become a continental meat-packing centre. In fact, the hinterland development which consolidated Calgary's position as a regional centre had little to do with the livestock industry and was probably detrimental to its growth.

It is typical of Calgary's inveterate optimism that the city's image-creating Stampede should be born in these dark days of the ranching industry. In an attempt to bolster the dying industry, the "Big Four" cattlemen put up the money in 1912 to finance promoter Guy Weadick's dream of a wild west show.[13] In a way, their boosterism was purely nostalgic. Fences had already tamed the open range, and time would soon cull the grizzled old cattlemen who had resisted them. But through the Stampede, Calgary came to symbolize cattle and the frontier to a degree that all the meat-packing plants in the West could never have done. It is a paradox of Calgary's history that its self-perpetuating image of cattle dependence originated in a time when the fruits of cash crop farming were everywhere evident in the city.

Fuelled by profits from successful agriculture, Calgary experienced rapid internal growth before 1914. Services and housing were expanded to meet the demands of a fast-growing regional and local population. Conditions were ideal for a flourishing construction industry, which drove land prices up and encouraged real estate speculation. City councils continued their inducement policies, which in 1912 culminated in the erection of the long-awaited CPR repair shops. During this time, money was plentiful. Bank interest rates remained at six per cent, unchanged since 1885, and loans were granted with a readiness that alarmed those of more conservative temper. Building contractors modified policies to allow easier repayment terms.[14] Despite these favourable circumstances, there was a perennial housing shortage in the city. The end result was the construction industry's vital role in Calgary's internal economic growth.

In its annual report for 1912, the Board of Trade noted its concern over the city's disproportionate reliance on the construction industry and found little satisfaction in the fact that Calgary was fourth on the North American continent in building construction. Such a revelation would have produced rapturous joy only a few years earlier. Calgary had over 200 listed contractors in 1912, while almost 25 per cent of the city's entire work force was employed directly in the construction industry in 1911. In the same year, there were more carpenters in Calgary than in any other occupation.[15] From 1910-12, almost $40 million were spent on construction in Calgary. Five hundred men worked on the construction of the Palliser Hotel in 1912. It later took 16 years (1915-30) for the number of building permits to total those issued for the three boom years 1910-12 (Appendix, Table XI). In 1913, one of Calgary's leading real estate men proudly told a California newspaper that a measure of the city's prosperity was evidenced by the fact that "you never hear the hammer stop . . . day or night".[16] In 1901, there were 1,689 houses in the city and the number had not doubled by 1907. By 1911, there were 11,350, and still demands could not be met. As early as 1908, over 40 million feet of lumber were needed for local construction. The largest brickworks in the city produced up to 80,000 bricks per day, while one storage shed had space for over one million bricks.[17]

As a result of the perennial housing shortage, building com-

The McAra and Walt Stationery Company, located on Seventh Avenue and First Street East, c. 1907.

panies began to specialize in houses for the working class, which, according to one concerned citizen, Calgary badly needed: "Many workmen have left the city because of inadequate housing. The shacks and tents in which people are living are worse than accommodation in the Ark."[18] These new construction companies were locally based and counted among their directors some of Calgary's most influential and successful promoters. In addition to housing construction, local money was active in financing the large business blocks, warehouses and other buildings which began to transform the physical face of Calgary by 1909.

Calgary's reliance on the construction industry was apparent in 1913, when the first effects of an economic recession hit the city. The construction companies were early casualties, with substantial lay-offs in 1913. Later, it was asserted that Calgary's solid enlistment record in the early years of the war was due primarily to members of the building trades who, out of work, had no alternative but to enlist.[19] Since the construction industry was a secondary component of internal economic growth, it merely reflected existing prosperity. The generating force had to come from other sources. In this respect, the disproportionate role of construction in Calgary's economy served to underscore unstable growth patterns in general.

The role of real estate speculation and investment in Calgary's economic growth is both complex and relevant to urban development in western Canada generally. On the one hand, real estate speculation reflected the measure of general confidence in the city's future. Certainly it was one of the most tangible manifestations of the booster rhetoric. On the other hand, solid investment in local real estate created a cash flow which stimulated internal economic growth, while activity in the real estate market generated jobs for many Calgary residents.

Land prices in Calgary escalated rapidly after 1909. There were accounts published daily of astronomical sums being paid for commercial sites. For example, Mrs. Fred Stimson bought the site of the York Hotel for $12,500 in 1907. In 1910, it sold for $100,000. This price escalation generated a speculative fever, and investors, large and small, gambled on commercial sites, residential lots and land parcels outside the city limits. Speculative frenzy peaked in 1912. The *Calgary Optimist*, virtually a real estate journal in those

years, summed up the general mood when it commented that any city's prosperity could be measured in terms of the number of resident real estate men.[20]

To a degree, the assertion in the *Optimist* was valid. Activity in real estate had stimulated the local economy. According to the 1911 census, over 440 licences were issued, and in the same year 2,000 people were employed actively in real estate. British, American and Canadian money flowed into the city as long-time property owners sold their holdings for large sums. It is also probable that much of the money invested in local business expansion originally came from lucrative land transactions. At least two of Calgary's more prominent merchants were originally real estate men. Albert A. Dick gradually abandoned his profitable real estate agency in favour of the construction business, and Edward H. Crandell branched into manufacturing with the Calgary Tent and Mattress Company. He was also sole owner of the Calgary Pressed Brick and Sandstone Company.[21]

Real estate speculation was tied to the booster mentality. When the boosters were quiet so was the real estate market. Promises of railway construction provided both promoters and land speculators with their chief rallying points. The frenzied speculation of 1909-12, which sent land prices soaring and stimulated the local economy, was linked to the proposed arrival in Calgary of the two transcontinental lines, the Canadian Northern and the Grand Trunk Pacific. As these lines approached the city limits, real estate activity and boosterism peaked. Downtown property sold for $3,000 per frontage foot, and land near the proposed railway terminals at the Mounted Police barracks and in the Mission area shot up to $1,000 per frontage foot.[22] The boosters on city council were also active, as city boundaries were extended towards the incoming lines and municipal debts soared on the guarantee of future prosperity. The failure of the two lines to affect Calgary as planned subdued the real estate market and the boosters for a long time.

Some of Calgary's most dynamic personalities during this period were real estate men.[23] Since almost every businessman of prominence dabbled more than occasionally in land dealings, the more aggressive real estate men were able to work reciprocal deals and move directly into building companies, mining concerns and other risk ventures in partnership with wealthy

The Eleventh Street office of C.C. Snowdon and Company, wholesale dealers in oil, 1911.

Christmas greetings from one of Pat Burns' retail butcher shops, 1909.

Pat Burns, on one of his Morgan saddle horses.

local figures. In this way, real estate men became an integral part of the business community. Many of them erected their own business blocks to promote their images and diversify their enterprises. One advertised a café on the roof of his proposed new building, "entirely enclosed in glass, elegantly appointed and beautified with exotics". The real estate men were embodiments of the booster mentality that characterized pre-1914 Calgary. Through their versatility and willingness to take risks, they typified the boundless optimism of urban Calgary. Indeed, when the real estate market tumbled in 1913-14, all were hurt but few were ruined. Most simply moved into the new speculative field of oil promotion.

Probably the most dynamic figure in the local business community during this period was real estate man and financial broker, Freddie C. Lowes.[24] He came west in 1903 as an employee of the Canada Life Assurance Company and entered the real estate business independently in 1905. By 1912, he had reached a pinnacle of financial success unprecedented in Calgary by a real estate agent. His holdings in southwest Calgary alone were conservatively estimated at over $2 million in 1911. Lowes' operations extended beyond Calgary, with offices throughout the United States and in Europe. In 1910, he completed the largest land deal ever transacted in Edmonton. Lowes opened the suburbs of Elbow Park, Glencoe and Roxborough in Calgary and sold the Ogden suburb, gratefully named Ceepeear, for a sum of $750,000. He made a fortune when commissioned by the Canadian Northern to buy up all land in Calgary along the railroad's proposed right-of-way.

Lowes was both practical and innovative. His scheme to use water pressure to wash away part of the Mission hill in preparation for a subdivision was considered quite an engineering feat at the time. As well as being a generous supporter of charitable causes, Lowes was an avid sportsman. His show horses were among Canada's best, and it is said that he held the record from Calgary to High River in an automobile. But this most successful of all local real estate men over-extended himself and was one of the casualties in the depression that followed the boom years. His financial and mental demise was a personal example of the uncertainties facing those who gambled everything on the future of urban centres in western Canada.

The importance of manufacturing continued to be reflected in city council policy. Water and light were supplied at cost to all establishments employing 20 people and spending $20,000.[25] Sites were readily obtainable on easy financial terms for up to $200 per acre, mainly in the Manchester subdivision which had been acquired by the city for manufacturing enterprises. The greatest incentive to manufacturing came in 1911, when the Horse Shoe Falls power project was completed. The question of cheaper power had bedevilled the various local governments for over 20 years. They had considered many alternatives, including natural gas and municipal power rights on the Elbow River,[26] before bowing to the financial muscle of the Calgary Power Company, formed under the guidance of Max Aitken (Lord Beaverbrook), Sir Herbert Holt, Richard Bedford Bennett and several local capitalists. The immediate need for cheaper power overrode all dissident voices. The *Calgary Optimist* wrote on December 11, 1909 that "we want to be a city . . . and we can't be at $80 per horse power." These rates were two and a half times those of Edmonton, Vancouver and Winnipeg. After the construction of the Horse Shoe project and the spirited bargaining between city and power officials, Calgary received its power for $30 per horse power.

The importance of cheap power to the city cannot be overestimated. In addition to an annual civic saving of $100,000, it enabled the development of the street railway system, which in turn dictated the direction and extent of physical growth. Cheap power attracted industries to Calgary and led local promoters to announce in 1910 that the new power supply, together with the discovery of mountains of iron ore 50 miles from Calgary, heralded the dawn of the "new Pittsburgh of the West". Most certainly the new source of cheap power influenced the CPR's decision to locate its repair shops in Calgary.

The construction of the Ogden Shops (1912-13) was easily the most important single contributing factor to economic growth within Calgary before the oil boom of the 1950s. City council had lobbied for their establishment ever since the CPR had indicated a need in western Canada for centralized repair facilities.[27] Medicine Hat, with its abundant supply of natural gas for cheap power, had considered its claim to the facilities to have priority. With the completion of the Horse Shoe project, the balance

Fred C. Lowes, in front of the Mission hill, which he had washed down by hydraulic pump to form the base of the Roxborough subdivision.

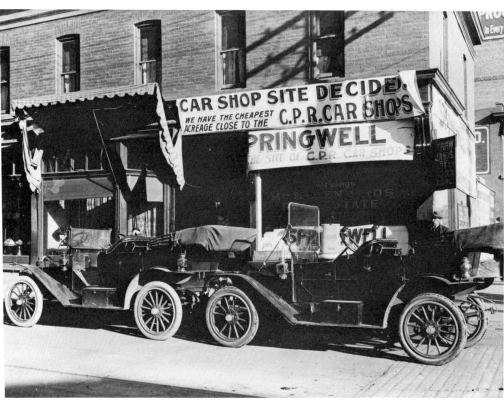

At the height of the land boom, McLaren Brothers' real estate office at Ninth Avenue and First Street West advertised acreage near the CPR Ogden location.

The CPR Ogden Shops, showing a modern crane at work in 1912. The establishment of these facilities was probably the greatest single stimulant to the city's economy before the oil boom of the 1950s.

tipped in Calgary's favour, and local concerns pressured the CPR. Members of the business community threatened a boycott of CPR services in favour of the anticipated Grand Trunk Pacific and Canadian Northern Railways. The civic authorities, however, adopted a more conciliatory stance by offering concessions for the shops. Under what became termed popularly as "The Ogden Agreement", the CPR consented to go ahead with the project while the city agreed to extend street railway services and absolve the railway from its obligations to construct underpasses in the downtown area. The construction of the shops took almost a year and employed almost 1,500. When completed, they were impressive structures. The locomotive sheds covered more than six acres, and future employment at the facilities was estimated at 5,000.[28] With the establishment of the Ogden facilities, Calgary achieved its dream of becoming a major railway centre.

During these years, Calgary's business community provided the city with aggressive leadership. Although firms based in eastern Canada, Winnipeg and United States were establishing branches in the city, control over economic development continued to devolve on Calgary residents. Excluding the Ogden shops, the largest manufacturing concerns were owned by local individuals. Calgary men drilled for natural gas in the district and within the city limits, and by 1913 a group of local businessmen had expressed interest in backing petroleum exploration in the Sheep Creek area southwest of the city. Calgary businessmen formed building companies and cooperatives designed to stimulate the construction industry. Countless mining and land development companies were organized during these years by local men seeking big dividends and undaunted by high-risk ventures. Private bridges were funded by local capital. Extensions to the street railway system were often underwritten by resident promoters. In short, most major decisions affecting Calgary's internal economic growth during these years were made in the offices of the major manufacturers, the Ranchmen's Club, the Board of Trade or city council.

The years 1910-12 marked an apex in Calgary's development. In economic terms, the future of the city was rosy and the general tenor of the business community was expansive. Rapid change and growth had given Calgary the hallmarks of urban prosperity, and its leaders were men with social and economic roots in the city. At this time, Calgary could hardly be classed as a financial or metropolitan centre, and the city had made little impact at the national level; but the initiative and formulae for growth and change had come from local sources. This self-determination, like the accompanying economic prosperity, was not to last. By 1913, Calgary was awash with depression, threats of war and unemployment. And though the autonomous role of Calgary's business leaders was to last longer, it was never again as strong as in those booming years of growth when Calgarians rode their city to the crests of prosperity.

POPULATION GROWTH AND ETHNIC RELATIONSHIPS

Extensive immigration after 1905 altered Calgary's population structure. Class distinctions became more observable as the socio-economic brackets widened, "better suburbs" appeared and workers' organizations proliferated. The city's British and eastern Canadian character was modified by the arrival of many Americans and Europeans. While the effects of these changes were reflected in new social customs and varying patterns of behaviour, more basic elements were unchanged. Anglo-Saxons remained dominant, and the right of property remained unchallenged.

As people moved into Calgary, the work force expanded and diversified. The socio-economic gaps between segments of the population widened. Differentiated districts and distinct patterns of social behaviour emerged as the city assumed characteristics traditionally associated with urban life. One aspect was the appearance of a substantial affluent class. In the 1890s, there were few wealthy individuals in Calgary. By 1912, they occupied whole subdivisions and counted millionaires among their number. The association of town and country wealth in the 1890s had given way to a new affluence that was clearly urban in orientation. In the frontier period there had been interaction between segments of society, but Calgary's pre-war elite had little contact with the average citizen. Recreational activities, entertainment, organizations and even hotels catered to different socio-economic groups. Golf at the new country club was an exclusive affair, as were the lavish parties given by the wealthy in the opulence of their city mansions. The rich attended symphony

Mrs. Jean McWilliam (third from left) with her daughter, hired girl and first boarders at her boarding house on Seventh Avenue near Paget Hall, 1911.

concerts and holy music recitals and listened to the sophisticated dialogue of daring new plays, even though some of them undoubtedly preferred slapstick vaudeville. Only the "best people" stayed at the Alberta Hotel. The wealthy were identified by their automobiles, their vacations away from the city and their fashionable tastes, select acquaintances and worthy social causes.

Calgary's elite tended to be imitative, and their upper-class trappings often appeared *gauche*. Their residences, for instance, were frequently exercises in architectural eclecticism. But it was this group's newness which fostered an enduring dynamic quality in Calgary. Upward social mobility was clearly attainable and, therefore, desirable. Although the affluent class of pre-1914 Calgary was young and unaccustomed to the mores of high social status, its very fluidity advertised the type of city emerging in the Alberta foothills. In the absence of tradition and heritage, entry to Calgary's upper class depended primarily on financial success.

It is difficult to assess how general prosperity affected the average person in Calgary. There are some indications that many lived a comfortable life. Hundreds of small, well-built bungalows were constructed during this period. Jobs were plentiful, and at the height of the boom the average family spent about half its income on staples.[29] Although organized labour did not become a potent force, it did achieve some success in regulating wages, particularly in the railway and building trades. The absence of heavy industry in Calgary precluded the emergence of a large unskilled labouring class. Most workers were skilled artisans or clerks, and average wages were higher than in more industrialized centres. There certainly seemed to be plenty of spending money. Newspapers carried scores of advertisements and notices of sales directed at the working class. Movie theatres were extremely popular and always crowded. There was also the speculation frenzy. Evidence suggests that many working men indulged in land speculation at the height of the boom in 1911-12.

But life was difficult for many people. Particularly after the collapse in 1913, when unemployment was high and relief measures were inadequate, labour began to enter municipal politics. Good wages were more than offset by the high price of staples. Many immigrants arrived in Calgary destitute, and each spring witnessed scenes of overcrowding and want. Rents were abnor-mally high during this whole period, while the housing shortage meant that many people lived in cramped quarters or in the confines of boarding houses. Poor districts emerged in east Calgary and outside the city limits where rents were low and taxes minimal. Private relief agencies often referred to the sorry state of families in which the breadwinner had either deserted or become sick or disabled.

The lot of the average individual in pre-1914 Calgary was comfortable only if he possessed good health and steady employment. He would be likely to save very little, if anything. And unless he possessed job security, he was subject to all the vicissitudes of economic uncertainty prevalent in a rapidly growing urban environment. For many, city life was too uncertain, and it was not unusual for a group of residents to ask the CPR to take over their properties and relocate them on farms.[30]

The flood of immigrants from the British Isles and Europe formed the nucleus of the labour force in Calgary. The census of 1911 showed that immigrants outnumbered native-born in every occupational category except the professions. They spilled into the city in increasing numbers after 1905, reaching a peak in 1911 when 56.1 per cent of Calgary's residents were foreign-born. However, it was the 19 per cent born in the United States and Europe which indicated that, despite continued Anglo-Saxon dominance, the basic structure of Calgary's population had been modified slightly (Appendix, Tables IV, V, VI, VII).

Germans comprised the largest single group of Europeans during this period. Numbering over 2,500 in 1911, they congregated on the flats north of the Bow River in the area that became known as Riverside or Germantown. A good number of the 900 immigrants from Austro-Hungary also lived in this area. Segregated both geographically and socially from the main business and residential sections of the city, these people lived in relative isolation. Many Germans were employed by the Riverside Lumber Company, owned by the Austrian-born Sereth brothers. Others worked at the brewery or in the manufacturing establishments across the river in the area aptly named Breweryville.

Riverside became the hub of German activity in Calgary. A Lutheran and Moravian church was opened in 1910. Teachers of German origin taught at Riverside and Bridgeland schools. The local Harmonic Club was distinctively German and established a

Jewish baseball team in Calgary, c. 1913.

tradition of German music in Calgary. Galicians of German origin formed a branch of the Socialist Party in 1908.[31] Although no Germans ran for municipal office during this period, candidates for civic elections actively sought the German vote, and at least one alderman owed his victory to his popularity with the Germans.[32]

Sharing the Riverside area with the Germans and Austro-Hungarians were the Italians. Although few in number, the Italians were strong in initiative and national pride. In 1907, after discovering that local flour made excellent macaroni, the Italian community formed the Alberta Macaroni Company and raised $5,000 to launch the project. Located initially on Third Avenue East, this company was more than a mere commercial enterprise. The factory also became a social centre. As the *Herald* reported on July 22, 1907:

> As visitors drew near to the building . . . the clear ring and swing of the mandolin accompanied by the strumming of a guitar could be plainly heard and the scraping feet of the dancers kept time to the music. The music was in the operating room of the factory.

The factory was still going two years later and appeared in city directories before 1914. In 1913, two Italians, one a former assistant *maître d'hôtel* at the Palliser Hotel and the other a sign artist with the municipal railway, organized a band which gave open air concerts and played in Stampede parades for over 20 years.

Only two other ethnic groups, the French and the Jews, numbered over 500 in these years. There had been a nucleus of French-speaking residents in Calgary since the freighting days of the 1870s. Initially, they lived in the area around the Roman Catholic mission and actually had their settlement incorporated as the village of Rouleauville in 1899. Later, a Métis community grew up west of the town in the area known as Shaganappi. A number of Jewish people, generally active in small businesses, also moved into Calgary. Unlike other ethnic groups, the Jews did not form distinct communities and were not as identifiable as other minority groups in the city.

Other European groups were too small to significantly modify Calgary's social character during this period. They preserved their common heritage through informal social gatherings and formed societies peculiar to their needs. Usually, they turned to the church for the institutional framework necessary to nurture their children in traditional values. They displayed their cultural individuality in the annual parades typical of the period. Thwarted by the language barrier and the lack of social acceptance, these ethnic groups made no inroads into the city's business and political power structures. Some change in this situation began in 1913, when Calgary offered adult courses in English for the foreign-born.[33]

The greatest number of immigrants to Calgary came from the British Isles, with many migrating on the advice of acquaintances who had already settled. It was this group which made the greatest contribution to the diversification of the work force. Most of the British immigrants chose to live near their places of work and congregated according to countries or areas of origin. There was a concentration of Welsh families in the working class suburb of Manchester, while Yorkshiremen lived in nearby Parkhill. Workers from County Durham settled in the railway suburb of Ogden. Some landowners tried to take advantage of quasi-national sentiments by naming their subdivisions to attract certain groups, such as the invitation to the Irish to live in Killarney or Belfast.

Immigrants from the United Kingdom maintained their identities by perpetuating social institutions from their homelands. The annual St. Patrick's Day and Orangemen's parades were well attended, though hardly popular with the local constabulary who had to handle the frequent disruptive incidents. Recreational clubs, sporting teams and cultural organizations brought Britishers together to share common pastimes and interests in this strange and somewhat primitive city.

American migration after 1905 had a considerable impact on the settlement pattern in western Canada. Between 1906 and 1911, thousands of Americans crossed the border into western Canada. They fostered improved farming techniques and stimulated urban growth. Unlike many other immigrants, Americans were seldom short of money when they reached Canada. In 1908, the promotional magazine *Prosperous Calgary* estimated that between 1906 and 1908 incoming Americans injected over $150 million cash into the national economy. By 1911, over 3,500 Americans lived in Calgary; generally, they were far more

Many residents of Chinese origin, such as the Hing Wah family shown here, were successful market gardeners in Calgary.

affluent and much more familiar with urban life than other immigrants. They were quickly assimilated into all echelons of society, and many became successful businessmen and social leaders. Some, like Charles Traumweiser, A. Judson Sayre and Herbert Anderson, were active in real estate and investment companies. American-owned companies, like the German-American Colonization Company and the Calgary Colonization Company, dealt in farmlands and city subdivisions. Edward Knape formed the Union Iron Works, and John Brookbank was chief executive for International Harvester in western Canada. There were also old-time American residents like Daniel Webster Marsh, mayor in 1889 and first president of the Western Stockgrowers' Association in 1896.

Perhaps the most interesting personality in Calgary during this period was the American James Wheeler Davidson of the Crown Lumber Company.[34] Davidson, a graduate of the Northwestern Military Academy in Illinois, was a member of Robert Peary's expedition to north Greenland in 1893-94. He was the author of four books on Formosa, war correspondent with the Chinese and Japanese armies in 1895-96 and a senior member of the American consulate in China during 1904-05. While in Calgary, Davidson became a leading figure in the North American Rotary movement. It was through the energies of property owners like Davidson and Sayre that Mount Royal became Calgary's most prestigious suburb. Certainly its soubriquet, "American Hill", gave an indication of the role of Americans in Calgary.

The Americans preserved their cultural identity in Calgary through social institutions based on models in the United States. These were nurtured through reciprocal visits with similar organizations in adjoining American states. The annual exhibition featured an American Day as part of the program. It was probably the noisiest day of the exhibition, with delegates from the United States arriving in force to show the locals "how it was done". Fourth of July celebrations were carried on enthusiastically in Victoria Park. The sight of a lone American flag draped across a car during the 1911 Coronation Day parade symbolized the presence of the only group in the city irreverent enough to mock the imperial tie.

It was during these years that Calgary assumed its very strong American character. The reasons for this cannot be directly attributed to the number of Americans in the city. Almost every western Canadian town counted many Americans among its residents, and in 1911 Edmonton had more Americans than Calgary. Calgary merely reflected the cultural impact of the United States that was being felt across the nation. Like other Canadian cities, Calgary received its first public library under a Carnegie Foundation grant. The local press followed the national example and gave extensive coverage to American news and sporting events. Cricket lost out to baseball and the magic appeal of the World Series. Numerous American entertainment troupes counted Calgary as only one of many stops in western Canada.

It was probably Calgary's association with cattle and the ranching industry which fostered a distinctly American flavour in the city. Many cattlemen were American ex-cowboys. Particularly after the Cyprus Hills area was opened to ranching in 1906, American-owned companies moved into southeast Alberta.[35] Local ranchers kept a close eye on the American cattle situation and made frequent trips to marketing centres in the United States. The cattletown image cultivated by Calgary boosters had definite American connotations, and the Calgary Stampede did much to enhance Calgary's cowtown image and further ties with the United States. The wild west atmosphere of the Stampede is essentially that popularized in American folklore. From its inception in 1912, when a cowboy band from Oregon led the parade and the meanest horse was an American import, the Stampede continued to reflect American influences. One could argue that up to 1950, at least, the cattle industry and the Stampede did more to cultivate an American image in Calgary than did the physical presence of Americans living in the city.

Restricted by immigration laws, the Chinese population[36] grew slowly during this period, and by the census of 1911 numbered 485. It was not until 1906 that the first child of Chinese parents was born in Calgary. The Christianization of Calgary's Chinese population began during these years. In 1901, Thomas Underwood had donated land and money for the erection of a Chinese mission on Tenth Avenue South. An assortment of businesses and commercial facilities sprang up in the area and became Calgary's first Chinatown. In addition to teaching Christian beliefs, the mission also conducted special English classes. 1911 marked the beginning of Chinese freemasonry in the city, and a national precedent was set in 1912 with the formation of an affiliated Chinese YMCA. Through these institutions, the Chinese began the long process of easing themselves into Calgary's dominant cultural milieu without forsaking their ethnic uniqueness.

By 1914, the Chinese had achieved economic independence if not social equality. Still dominating the laundry trade, they were also moving into restaurant and market garden businesses that continued to expand and compete successfully with other commercial enterprises. Many owned land and businesses, and a few had acquired positions of affluence and status in Calgary's business world. Their commercial establishments were thriving, and market gardens were expanding into greenhouse operations. Chinese leaders demonstrated a willingness to support civic programs and public fund-raising campaigns. In short, the Chinese appeared willing to accept Calgary, even if Calgary still refused to accept them.

Calgary remained staunchly Anglo-Saxon during these years, more so than Winnipeg or Edmonton, where greater cultural diversification was evident. Although many European immigrants passed through Calgary between 1905 and 1912, most headed north to the parklands of central Alberta. In Calgary, as in other western Canadian cities, Britain was still regarded as a major source of capital investment, ideas and institutional structures. The difference in Calgary was essentially numerical. With non-Anglo-Saxons numbering less than 15 per cent of the population in 1911, there was little chance that dominant social elements would be modified by the "melting pot". Because of this numerical dominance, social disequilibrium was often predicated upon ethnic distinctions. Of all foreign groups, non-Anglo-Saxons were the most deprived socially and economically. Labour was hostile towards Asiatics and Europeans. In 1911, for instance, Calgary cooks struck to protest the employment of Chinese labour in restaurants. The press was critical of European minorities and often associated their presence with squalor and poverty. Because of their small number, Calgary's non-Anglo-Saxon minorities were at least as wretched and probably more isolated than those in cities like Winnipeg, where ethnic cosmopolitanism was more in evidence.

THE URBAN LANDSCAPE

The physical appearance of Calgary changed markedly under the influence of rapid growth. The business centre grew, with many buildings reaching six storeys, the maximum height allowed under city bylaw. This restriction was not rooted in aesthetics, but was typically pragmatic. Water pressure was insufficient to guarantee effective fire fighting in higher buildings. Exceptions were made for the Grain Exchange building and the Palliser Hotel, Calgary's first skyscrapers. Calgary's retail district extended along Eighth and Seventh Avenues between Third Street East and Second Street West, and the intersection at Eighth Avenue and First Street West became the heart of the city. The residential districts extended mainly south and west to Seventeenth Avenue and beyond to Roxborough, Elbow Park, Sunalta and Bankview. Settlement was slower on the north hill, although Crescent Heights, which was incorporated as a village in 1908 and annexed to the city in 1910, was a popular area. Manufacturing districts were centred in the east and in newly acquired locations near the Macleod Trail. In appearance and function, Calgary had become a small city (see Map 4).

Manufacturing land use followed precedents set in the 1880s with locations near railways or main roads in the east and southeast of the city. Sites were chosen with a view towards later expansion. However, there were some problems with the municipal policies governing manufacturing land use. Residential areas were encouraged within manufacturing districts, and no change occurred in the use of land along river banks.

The city's greatest success in directing land-use patterns resulted from the industrial policy of 1911, which outlined procedures that were followed with reasonable consistency. The overall result of the municipal policy was the consolidation of manufacturing enterprises in suitable locations with adequate provision for future expansion. Since its building bylaw did not provide for purely industrial districts, the city included inducements in its industrial policy, but these were limited by provincial statute. The city was to purchase suitable industrial areas, and industries were then attracted to these districts through the extension of uniform concessions. Since the city was able to provide utility and transportation services, the municipally owned areas were more attractive than privately owned properties. Indeed, the loudest objections came from those landholders who had hoped to profit from sales to prospective manufacturers.[37] Other factory owners complained that the city's uniform concession policies depreciated land values elsewhere in the city. Nevertheless, the industrial policy of 1911 gradually moved manufacturing concerns from high-rent locations to sites in designated industrial areas. Low-rent areas such as those along the Bow River remained untouched.

The city's choice of locations for industrial sites dictated future trends. Large areas were selected along the railways heading north to Edmonton and south to Fort Macleod. Manchester, the city's main industrial area, which was brought into the city limits by special provincial enactment, is in an unsightly trough of land between the railroad and the Macleod Trail. Adjacent areas fell into the hands of speculators. In 1912, Pat Burns sold land near Manchester to developers for $1.7 million. By bringing Manchester into the city limits, the civic policy-makers forestalled the possibility of manufacturers locating outside the corporate limits in order to avoid taxes.

The city encouraged the erection of workmen's houses near the industrial areas. Sometimes the city's purchase of property for industrial sites was contingent upon subsequent land being made available for residential purposes. Urban planners were convinced of the need to design residential subdivisions which would form a whole with the industrial areas they served.[38] The development of Ogden reinforced the notion of differentiation by district rather than by land use, and Manchester and Bonnybrook helped establish a pattern of isolated residential enclaves in areas which became increasingly industrial.

This period was also characterized by a continuation of the prevailing attitudes towards land use along the right bank of the Bow River. Declining land values reflected council's poor opinion of this area. The decision to allow the Chinese to remain in 1910 was undoubtedly linked to pessimistic attitudes towards the future of this part of the city. Most saw the area as suitable only for railway construction. In 1910, the proposed market site was located beside the river because of trackage considerations. Two years later when the Grand Trunk Pacific purchased the NWMP barracks ground, the site of old Fort Calgary, and ran its rails along the river edge to its proposed terminal, the city gave wholehearted approval. Although there were voices of concern over the future of an area high in scenic potential, any suggestions for beautification programs met with lukewarm response and meagre results. By 1914, the pattern of heterogeneous land use between the business area and the Bow River was firmly established.

Probably the most dominant factor in determining the growth of differentiated districts was the street railway system inaugurated in 1909. Within three years, there were over 50 cars traversing almost 60 miles of track. By this time, Calgary subdivisions sprawled more than 10 miles from the city centre, and the prime mover in this phenomenal suburban growth was the streetcar.

The street railway system reflected limitations imposed by both the railroad and topography. The CPR determined access routes from the south to the city centre when it constructed underpasses under its mainline. Since population concentration was in the southwest, these underpasses created bottlenecks which underscored the CPR's folly in opting for a townsite north of the tracks. Topographical factors also influenced streetcar routes. Rails were laid up Tenth Street North rather than Centre Street, where steep grades imposed special problems. The deep Shaganappi coulee effectively blocked extensions into the area west of Bankview and Sunalta, and the areas of Killarney and Altadore were accessible only when rails were laid up Fourteenth Street to circumvent the meandering Elbow River.

The street railway made commercial enterprises feasible beyond the city centre, particularly along Seventeenth Avenue South, Kensington Road, Tenth and Fourth Streets North and Eleventh Street South. Rents were appreciably lower here, and clusters of small one-owner and family establishments began to appear around the major intersections. However, the end of the boom in 1913-14 and the curtailment of streetcar extensions delayed the emergence of well-defined suburban commercial centres.

The street railway greatly influenced the growth of residential districts. Prospective homebuilders gravitated towards areas close to the streetcar routes. The CPR's decision to come to Ogden in 1911 was contingent upon street railway construction. Although a working class residential area was established adja-

Calgary's first streetcar, with civic officials in the foreground. The mayor of Calgary in 1909, Reuben R. Jamieson, is at right. Effectively delineating the extent of residential growth, Calgary's street railway system grew rapidly. Beginning with only two cars in 1909, it expanded to 70 cars operating on 71 miles of track by 1915. In December 1950, Calgary's streetcars made their last official runs, ending 41 years of service.

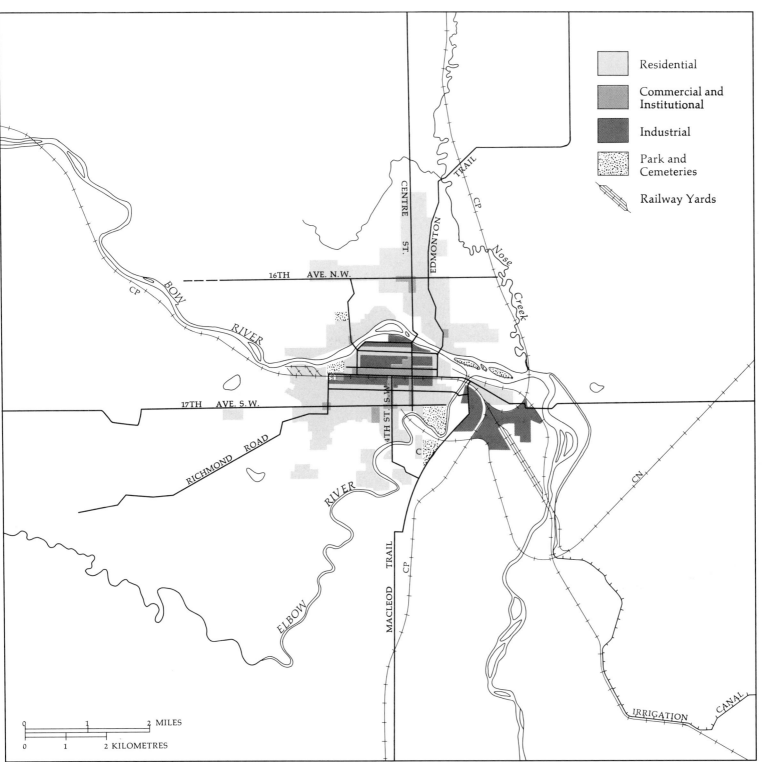

4

**Land Use
in Calgary,
1911**

Residential

Commercial and
Institutional

Industrial

Park and
Cemeteries

Railway Yards

CENTRE ST.

EDMONTON TRAIL

16TH AVE. N.W.

CP

Nose Creek

BOW

CP

RIVER

17TH AVE. S.W.

4TH ST. S.W.

RICHMOND ROAD

RIVER

C

CN

ELBOW

MACLEOD TRAIL

CP

IRRIGATION CANAL

0   1   2 MILES

0   1   2 KILOMETRES

The Palliser Hotel, 1910. Located next to the CPR station, the Palliser was to dominate Calgary's skyline for almost half a century.

Calgary's city hall was probably the most controversial building ever erected in the city. The new city hall was under construction for several years (the cornerstone reads 1907) and was officially opened in 1911 by the leader of the Opposition, Robert L. Borden. The building's $300,000 price tag was twice the original estimate and required a raise in the city's mill rate. Calgary's first city hall was a two-storey wooden building completed in 1887 at a cost of $1,694 on a site immediately west of the new building.

Calgary Public Market, 1912. Note the ever popular awning to the left.

cent to the shops, many workmen commuted from other parts of the city. In the inner areas, the street railway not only outlined main concentrations of population, but also became a positive instrument of public policy. Schools, apartments and boarding houses were always close to streetcar connections.

However, in the outlying areas the street railway became a tool of the land speculators. Because of successful efforts by developers in negotiations with the city for streetcar extensions, the districts of Tuxedo Park, Pleasant Heights, Killarney and Elbow Park gained early prominence as residential areas. Even the village of Forest Lawn outside the city owed its existence to the street railway. Originally intended as an intensive industrial area along the Grand Trunk Pacific line, Forest Lawn attracted the interest of developers who sold lots on the guarantee of street railway facilities.

The speculators' success in securing street railway connections to their holdings led to an over-extension of the system. The Shouldice-Bowness agreements provide excellent examples.[39] In 1910, city council agreed to extend streetcar services beyond the city limits to an area known as Shouldice Terrace in return for a 100-acre parcel of land for park purposes. In 1911, John Hextall, an Englishman who dreamed of fine Old Country-style mansions nestled in the Bow Valley, paid over $200,000 for 1,724 acres, which he named Bowness Park Estates. A company was formed for the purpose of selling one- and two-acre plots to wealthy Englishmen. Hextall proceeded to build a bridge across the Bow River for $75,000, an electric light plant for $125,000 and a pumping station for over $90,000. A golf course, designed by one of Britain's leading golf architects, was laid out and a clubhouse erected at a contract price of $28,000. Even the *Financial World* was impressed. After warning its readers of the dangers of investing in subdivided property without special assurances, the *Financial World* went on to discuss the merits of Hextall's property: "Houses erected thereon are from $5,000 to $33,000 each in cost and it is believed that within one year every lot will be worth double or triple its present value."[40] The city council was impressed by Hextall's promises and in 1911 he secured assurance that the Shouldice streetcar extension would be continued to Bowness in return for a donation of two islands in the Bow River.[41]

The Bowness car line became notorious as it rumbled, almost empty, across the bald prairie carrying milk from dairies to the city. Although the islands, today known as Bowness Park, proved to be a great success as a scenic attraction, the residential district did not develop as Hextall had dreamed. He died before most of his subdivided land reverted to acreage. By 1913, the city's folly in extending streetcar service to Shouldice and Bowness was apparent. Shouldice Park was described as a site for drunken parties, while less than a year later the Bowness car line was labelled "a white elephant".[42] But since construction costs were relatively low, land speculators often built their own street railway lines linking subdivisions to the city's system. They then donated these lines to be operated by the city. Since civic officials could rarely refuse such gifts, the result was unplanned expansion of Calgary's street railway network. This expansion led to the needless extension of corporate boundaries, the wider dispersal of population and the emergence of poorer residential districts in outlying areas.

The emergence of differentiated residential districts during this period showed the municipal government and private developer in distinct yet complementary roles. For while Calgary's growth appeared to be unplanned, the influence of both public and private policy was discernible. Residential districts were differentiated according to three criteria: the presence of the streetcar, utility services and stringent building restrictions. Natural topographic advantage was not a paramount concern. Exclusive districts possessed all three features, but the extension of utility services was the area in which municipal decisions were most crucial. Unlike street railway extensions, the provision of utilities was very costly and lagged far behind residential construction. Municipal authorities, by allocating priority to utility extensions, actually determined the type of district which developed.

With regard to the overall standard of dwellings, the City of Calgary possessed neither the power nor the inclination to control development. The building bylaw of 1912, the city's first such statute, was fairly lenient in regulating construction. The 25-foot frontage lot was encouraged even though its undesirability was already apparent. Indeed, such lots were very popular, for they appealed to a wide range of purchasers and allowed intensive settlement. Loose regulations governing size and placement of

Home of H.A. Christensen at 3207 Sixth Street S.W., c. 1913. The woman's enormous hat was considered very fashionable.

buildings often resulted in diverse structures on the same block.

Although many subdivisions were poorly laid out, developers easily secured approval from city councils hoping to ease the acute housing shortage and acquire additional taxation revenue. In 1907, the provincial Minister of Public Works, William H. Cushing, remarked on Calgary: "Some very peculiar work is being done in connection with subdividing property . . . . I have here before me one subdivision plan . . . and it is one of the worst subdivisions I have ever seen."[43] Cushing, a long-time Calgary resident and businessman, was under no illusions about land development practices in the city.

Throughout this period, city councils remained committed to growth, even though provincial legislation embodied in the Town Planning Act of 1912 was intended to curb indiscriminate speculation. The Calgary concept of controlled development adhered more to the grand design of British planner Thomas Mawson, who, in 1914, prepared an elaborate plan for directing the city's growth. At the time, councils appeared satisfied that adequate differentiation was provided in the building bylaw and the policies of individual developers. Ostensibly, developers made contracts with buyers determining the types of dwellings to be erected. But because neither the developer nor the city could enforce these "contracts", areas such as the Lindsay Estate featured haphazard growth patterns. Scenically located on a rise south and east of the Elbow River, this subdivision was intended to cater to a "better class" of resident. Instead, some buyers refused to honour their commitments and erected sub-standard dwellings. When the owner tried to persuade the city to withhold building permits, the city revealed its legal impotence in such matters.

Some developers were successful in enforcing building restrictions. Easily the best results were in the subdivision known as Mount Royal, owned by the CPR and handled by the prominent firm of Toole, Peet and Company. Substantial building restrictions were strictly enforced with the result that Mount Royal became Calgary's first truly exclusive subdivision. Huge mansions were set in spacious lots on specially contoured thoroughfares. Residents guarded their interests through the Mount Royal Improvement Association. This organization was headed by the most powerful real estate men in the city, who, having

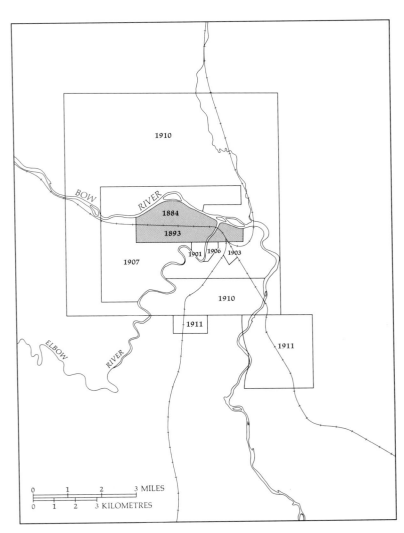

5 Boundary Extensions, 1884-1911

The home of William Roper Hull at 1202 Sixth Street S.W., in the early 1900s. Hull Estates apartment block now stands on this site. The tall chimneys of the Roper house and the use of sandstone brick with trim show a familiarity with late Victorian styles. As a prominent member of Calgary's business and social communities, Hull often entertained with large parties on the landscaped lawns of his city home and at the Hull Ranch.

built residences in Mount Royal, were determined to keep it a haven for the privileged few. To the south along the Elbow River, Freddie Lowes used building restrictions and extensive land improvements to make his subdivision among the most desirable in the city.

The subdivisions in Mount Royal and along the Elbow River established the southwest as Calgary's elite residential area. The north hill continued to attract modestly priced residences. After the privately owned Centre Street bridge failed to attract sizeable settlement and developers failed to promote Tuxedo Park as a luxury suburb, real estate men lost interest in the north hill and concentrated their energies on the southwest.

One characteristic of the period was the prevailing notion that Calgary was destined for big city status. The city's population was expected to reach 100,000 by 1920. The need to consolidate a big city downtown area led to the erection of buildings in violation of height restrictions. City council's approval of remote subdivisions and the extension of streetcar services beyond reasonable residential settlement typified official boom euphoria. Speculative activity increased outside the city limits, spurred on by the promise of railway construction. At this time, the Inter-Urban Railway Company was conceived as an electric train network bringing Calgary a daily delivery of produce from neighbouring rural centres. Since its proposed route into Calgary was never clearly defined, many land transactions were made on rumour. Although the two transcontinental lines provided a more substantial base for speculation, the timing of their actual entry into Calgary was conjectural. Speculators also acquired land to persuade the city to purchase future industrial sites outside the corporate limits. Given the poorly defined municipal policies of the period, it was not difficult for speculators to convince local authorities that a bigger city and increased tax revenues would be beneficial. The result was the growth of Calgary to over 36 square miles by 1912 (see Map 5).

THE URBAN COMMUNITY: SOCIAL AND POLITICAL LIFE

In many respects, the nature of local government had remained unchanged since the frontier days. High property qualifications for the positions of mayor, aldermen and commissioner excluded poorer residents from holding office. The municipal franchise restricted the vote to owners of property worth $200 or tenants on premises worth $400. But the emergence of differentiated districts and an electoral ward system did contribute to more heterogeneous councils. Particularly in the northern and eastern areas of the city, candidates for civic office became more sensitive to the working class vote.

A major change in the structure of local government occurred in 1909, when elected commissioners assumed the responsibilities previously held by the standing committees. The growing complexity of civic administration had indicated a need for restructuring, and the question of commission government had been debated sporadically in council for years. Although the decision to elect commissioners revealed a general desire to exercise democratic privileges, it did not mean that the administration of civic affairs was in more efficient hands than under the old standing committees. One of the first commissioners in 1909 was Simon John Clarke, ex-Mounted Policeman and saloon owner, who had had no experience in municipal politics since 1885. Other early commissioners were more noted for their enthusiasm and diligence than they were for their administrative abilities.

Another development which modified the operation of local government was the interjection of the province into municipal affairs. The Town Planning Act of 1912 instructed municipalities to take steps to provide for orderly and planned growth. In the same year, an amendment to the Land Titles Act stated that provincial approval was needed for subdivisions in municipalities. In 1913, further legislation was enacted prohibiting municipalities from granting bonuses or providing tax exemptions to industrial establishments.

Municipal ownership of utilities made headway with the introduction of a city-owned street railway system in 1909 and the construction of a municipal paving plant in 1912. Both were profitable ventures in these years. A gravity waterworks on the Elbow River was built after $340,000 was allotted in 1907. Although this system proved inadequate, it usually returned a surplus and served to sustain a faith in municipal ownership. It was Calgary's experience with the natural gas utility that shook public confidence in private ownership of essential services.

The natural gas controversy which continued in Calgary until

Eugene Coste, ''the father of the natural gas industry in western Canada''. A well-known geologist and engineer, Coste discovered natural gas in the Bow Island field near Lethbridge in 1908. Gas from this field supplied Calgary from 1912 until the early 1920s.

Archibald Wayne Dingman was head of Calgary Petroleum Products, the company whose strike in the Turner Valley on May 14, 1914 set off a frenzy of oil speculation and ushered in Calgary's future as an oil and gas centre.

Bricklayers and Masons Union, Local 2, at a Labour Day parade in Calgary, 1906.

The construction crew who worked on Calgary's public library in 1911.

FIRST BAPTIST CHURCH
CALGARY
APRIL 1906,
B244

COPYRIGHT
ERNEST BROWN

Calgary First Baptist Church on the northeast corner of Seventh Avenue and First Street West. This building was constructed at a cost of $22,569 after a fire in 1905 destroyed the old church on the same site. Opened in August 1905, the new church soon became the centre of an expanding ministry.

the 1940s had its roots in the city's early encouragement of private utility monopolies. In 1903 and 1905, exclusive franchises were granted to two locally controlled companies, one to manufacture artificial and the other to produce natural gas. The more significant of the two was the natural gas company, headed by Archibald Dingman of later petroleum fame and backed by local businessmen. After drilling unsuccessfully on the Sarcee Indian Reserve from 1906 to 1908, the Calgary Natural Gas Company moved to the estate of Major James Walker in east Calgary. Here, a considerable gas flow was discovered at 2,000 feet — 500,000 to 1,000,000 cubic feet daily. Dingman's company supplied small quantities of gas to the city, serving the brewery and lighting streets in east Calgary. In 1912, the recently formed Canadian Western Natural Gas Heat and Power Company Ltd., headed by Eugene Coste, secured leases on CPR lands near Bow Island. On July 17, 1912, natural gas reached Calgary through a 170-mile pipeline in quantities large enough to supply the city's needs.

In 1911, Dingman had transferred his company's assets and the franchise to service the city to Coste. A year later, Coste's company was claiming the exclusive right to distribute gas in Calgary. By November 1912, city council was expressing displeasure over the high price of gas and the consequent discouragement of industrial growth. In September 1914, when the city decided to test the gas company's monopoly in the courts, the *Herald* referred to a "declaration of municipal war". The following February, council announced it would invite outside tenders to supply gas, pending a favourable legal decision. But in an appeal, the court ruled that the Canadian Western Natural Gas Company had exclusive rights by franchise.[44] The Dingman franchise did not become statutory until 1926, when the city received the right, after an 11-year interim, to expropriate with a view towards establishing a city-owned utility.

The profitable and orderly management of city-owned utilities stood in sharp contrast to the bitter battle over Coste's natural gas monopoly. During this period, Calgary firmly established its faith in municipal ownership. When the first Labour candidate was elected to city council in 1915, at the height of the natural gas controversy, his main platform called for municipal ownership of all utilities.[45]

At this time, the personality of organized labour was elitist and hardly conducive to working class solidarity.[46] The local Trades and Labour Council was dominated by the building trades, and bricklayers, stonemasons and carpenters, zealously pursuing their own interests, were often in open conflict with each other. This lack of solidarity was evident in the unsuccessful carpenters' strike of 1903 and in the 1911 labour dispute at the city hall construction site.[47] However, the sustained construction boom enabled these unions to better their collective lot in comparison with other members of the labouring classes, particularly the newly arrived immigrant to whom the Trades and Labour Council was openly hostile. In 1911, carpenters walked off the job rather than work with a Black,[48] while other unskilled immigrant workers lived and worked in wretched conditions. In 1907, it was estimated that local postal workers existed on little more than a subsistence wage.[49]

Politically, organized labour in Calgary, with its craft guild consciousness, was more in tune with traditional practices than with any emerging radical sentiment. Labour candidates in provincial and federal elections received scant support in the city. Conservative R.B. Bennett probably enjoyed the support of organized labour during his successful federal campaign in 1911.[50] In local politics, two individuals associated with the labour movement were elected to council, but neither could be classed as a labour representative in the accepted sense. Richard A. Brocklebank, a one-time president of the local carpenters' union, was manager of Thomas Underwood's extensive construction operations. And although Calgary's wartime mayor Michael Costello had been a union executive, he was also a medical doctor and did not campaign as a labour representative.

The restricted franchise, general prosperity and disharmony among unions all militated against labour's entry into municipal politics on an organized basis. Instead, the local Trades and Labour Council persuaded city councils to give favourable treatment to unionized local workers. In 1909, labour representatives secured a verbal promise from the city to hire only local men, and in 1913, council adopted a resolution stipulating that contractors with the city pay union rates to their employees. A year earlier, a divided council had appropriated $1,000 to form a Labour Bureau to deal with unemployment.

The development of organized labour and its attitude towards management and politics represented an extension more than a re-definition of the frontier mentality. In spite of increasing union activity in the city, self-interest and parochialism continued to transcend any nascent class consciousness. Common interests went no further than an awareness of the principle of unionism. Though the potential of organized labour as a political force was recognized, it was not a factor during this period. Labour was decidedly apathetic towards the 1913 plebiscite which abolished the ward system.[51] With the election of aldermen from the city at large, the emerging working class districts were denied the distinct political identity which may have helped fuse the voice of organized labour in Calgary.

In federal politics, Calgary remained solidly Conservative, and the city rejoiced when the Conservatives returned to power in 1911. Cattlemen had been soured by the Liberal Party's lease policies, which they felt were ruining the range industry, and by the failure of their lobbying efforts to win preferred legislation in Ottawa. Furthermore, they maintained that by encouraging agriculture at all costs, the Liberals would foster grain growing in areas suitable only for grazing.[52] The Liberal Party's railway policies also came under criticism in Calgary. The fact that both transcontinental lines were to pass through Edmonton hinted of a familiar Edmonton-Liberal plot. Even when both companies disclosed plans to build branch lines to Calgary, local business-men and politicians remained sceptical.

The election of 1911 also accentuated Calgary's growing urban status. The reciprocity debate had clearly shown the Liberal Party as representing rural interests and the Conservatives as being more urban in focus.[53] Calgary's solid endorsement of Conserva-tive R.B. Bennett in a by-election held in the city in October 1911 could be interpreted as both a traditional rejection of the Liberals and an awareness of increased urban status. Certainly Bennett's overwhelming victory could not be attributed to his own personal popularity. Two years earlier, he had been defeated by William H. Cushing in a provincial election. Cushing, Calgary's sole provincial member from 1905 until his resignation amid the rail-way scandal of 1910, was elected despite his Liberal affiliations and because of his integrity and personal popularity.

On the provincial level, Calgary entered a long period of politi-cal impotence. By 1913, the Liberals were still in solid control,

with 38 members in the 56-seat legislature. Calgary had three members in the House. All were Conservatives and all were elected with handsome majorities. In addition to the increasing identification of the Liberal Party with rural sentiments, the loss of the university for Calgary, coming so soon after the bitter capital dispute, did much to shatter Liberal credibility in Calgary.

After Edmonton was named provincial capital, people in Cal-gary generally believed that the provincial university, when established, would be located in the city. In the first session of 1905, an act to establish and incorporate a university was intro-duced by Hon. Alexander C. Rutherford, premier and minister of education. Two years later, provision was made for the purchase of a site, and over the strenuous objections of William H. Cush-ing, 258 acres were obtained on the south side of the Saskatche-wan River in Strathcona, the premier's constituency. Calgarians were infuriated. They felt the provincial government had acted arrogantly and irresponsibly. On April 6, 1907, the *Daily News* in Calgary commented bitterly that "the system of hogging to Edmonton everything of material benefit will have to be departed from". It seemed that the premier had allowed personal interests to interfere with his role as chief elected official in the province. The Liberal editor of the *Albertan*, William M. Davidson, wrote in 1913: "One man is to blame and one man only for the Provincial University not being in Calgary. That man is A.C. Rutherford!"[54]

Calgary's fight for a university was not over yet. In 1909, a movement to establish a university in Calgary was initiated by Dr. Thomas H. Blow, a local physician with a concern for the future of higher education in Calgary. Land was donated for a site west of the city in an area described as being the same elevation as Mt. Vesuvius.[55] A total of 750 acres was given, most by William J. Tregillus, who was active in local political circles and the infant United Farmers of Alberta. Up to $100,000 cash, including a donation of $25,000 from Lord Strathcona, was raised by 1912 for the university endowment, and due mainly to the efforts of Dr. Blow, Calgary College was incorporated and actually held classes in the public library in the fall of 1912. Unfortunately, it had no degree-granting powers, and after failing to have the college affiliated with Queens University, Dr. Blow, now a Conservative member of the Legislative Assembly, petitioned the provincial government to establish a commission to enquire into and re-

Riverside Public School, c. 1911. Erected in 1909, it is now called Langevin Junior High School.

Boxing was a major attraction in early Calgary. The 1913 fight between Arthur Pelkey (third from right) and Luther McCarthy was hailed as the biggest match ever promoted in the city, and a special arena was built in the Manchester subdivision. The fight went on despite a neck injury sustained by McCarthy a few days earlier. In the first round McCarthy was knocked down by a light blow to the head. He died within minutes.

Women playing tennis at the Calgary Lawn Tennis Club in Scarborough, c. 1913.

port upon procedures contained in the bill respecting Calgary College. In February 1915, after 16 months of deliberations, the commission recommended the establishment of a Provincial Institute of Technology and Art in Calgary and voted against giving Calgary College the power to grant degrees.

The erosion of confidence in the Alberta Liberal Party meant that Calgary mirrored federal voting patterns at the provincial level. It also contributed to the emergence of Calgary as a political adversary to Edmonton. During this period, Calgary became the Alberta headquarters of the rural protest movement which was gaining national momentum. Also based in Calgary was the recently organized United Farmers of Alberta which, during these years, began building the organization that would topple the Liberals from provincial power in 1921.

The most significant aspect of Calgary's social growth during this period was the proliferation of services usually associated with urban life. An increased emphasis on efficiency led to more formalized structures. Social services were institutionalized in keeping with current practice and philosophy. Some services were organized to alleviate social distress; others provided solely for the recreational needs of a fast-growing population.

Between 1906 and 1914 significant changes occurred in Calgary's public school system.[56] A full-time superintendent was appointed in 1906, and a provincial normal school was in operation by 1908. By 1914, 34 school buildings housed 7,451 pupils and 198 teaching staff. The phenomenal growth of Calgary's public school system reflected the impersonal and bureaucratic educational model of the big city. It provided an excellent example of the effect of the urban mentality on an institution which did not belong primarily to an urban setting.

The reorganization of the police force really began in 1909, when tough but unconventional Chief Tom English was dismissed. English's unorthodox methods had always disturbed those who wanted a more up-to-date police force. Prostitution and drug use were widespread by this time, and there was a need for a "big-city" police chief to expand the modest force of 27, with its operating budget of less than $30,000. By 1914, a 96-man police force, under the direction of ex-Toronto inspector Alfred Cuddy, had done much to modernize police work in Calgary, and not a single drug case was reported in that year. Improved

communications were a big factor in the reduced crime rate. The expanded force had a patrol wagon, four sub-stations and 33 Ganewell police boxes. A mounted section had been established and an identification bureau was in operation by 1913. The annual budget for the police force in 1914 was almost $160,000, more than five times the 1909 budget and an indication of Calgary's willingness to pay the costs of modern and efficient law enforcement.

In other areas, Calgary's urban growth was characterized by organized efforts to provide wider services and to deal with specific areas of social distress. Special facilities existed by 1914 to handle alcoholism, tuberculosis and smallpox. A children's shelter, under the auspices of city council and the Children's Aid Society, provided for needy, neglected or abandoned children. A modern library with over 7,000 volumes was opened to the public in 1912. Although city council only gave $2,000 to the associated charities in 1911, this figure represented a fourfold increase within two years. Both the YMCA and the YWCA were established in Calgary, catering especially to the many homeless young adults who drifted in and out of the city seeking work.

Other organizations began to pressure local government on various issues. The Board of Trade, the Retail Merchants Association and the labour organizations were active. The Rotary Club led the early closing movement in 1915, while the Humane Society was concerned over council's neglect of stray animals. However, the various women's organizations were probably the most active in pressuring civic governments and in leading the movements towards social reform. As advocates of social improvement, women had traditionally been active in Calgary. Many women had signed the various petitions to councils in the 1880s and 1890s complaining of health hazards and social evils. Women led the movement which resulted in the construction of Calgary's first hospital in 1895. Later, the Women's Hospital Aid Society made substantial contributions towards the provision of a maternity wing and a nurses' residence.

The social abuses which accompanied Calgary's rapid population growth quickened the activities of the already dynamic female reform groups. Calgary's YWCA was established in 1910 in spite of official disinterest and a degree of male scepticism.[57] Women led the agitation which resulted in Carnegie funds for a

Robert C. Edwards, editor of the Calgary Eye Opener.

Hillhurst Presbyterian Sunday school group crusading for temperance on Kensington Road.

public library.[58] The Society for Sanitary and Moral Prophylaxis was formed in 1909 under female direction to study issues such as venereal disease and hygiene, and in 1912 various women's groups pressured council to take action to censor moving pictures being shown in the city.[59] The local branch of the Women's Christian Temperance Union was interested in using the growing female municipal franchise, estimated at 1,600 in 1912. Following the narrow passage of a bylaw authorizing the construction of a malting company, the WCTU began exploring ways to marshal the female vote effectively. In 1913, a Women's Consumer League was formed to combat rising prices and to complain about the shortage of fresh products. This organization, 1,000 strong, attempted to influence city council to change the bylaws regarding short weight and other infractions.[60] Other women's groups sought to break down social barriers. The Women's Canadian Club attempted to ease racial prejudice by inviting non-Anglo-Saxon speakers. Similarly, the International Sunshine Club appealed to women everywhere to work towards "general harmony".

The significance of the various women's organizations and the other social bodies active in Calgary during this period was twofold. First, most of these organizations, as branches of national and international bodies, served to direct general concerns into a local context. Secondly, their presence in Calgary indicated that the city was able to accommodate and nurture groups whose activities reflected the mainstream of urban social thought.

Many of Calgary's social organizations functioned in a narrow context with specific goals. They worked towards prescribed ends, and their voice of protest was more practical than idealistic, more concerned with individual problems than with general ills. But Bob Edwards, the crusader, was a new kind of voice and the spokesman for general reform. He was essentially a product of an urban environment, finding both his subject matter and his audience in the city. No place seemed able to hold this restless spirit but Calgary, to which he came from his native Scotland via France, the United States, a host of Alberta towns and Winnipeg. Only in Calgary did he find that blend of frontier egalitarianism and social disequilibrium which could tolerate and sustain his acerbic pen.

Bob Edwards[61] was a brilliant journalist and editor of the *Eye Opener*, which appeared intermittently in Calgary from 1904 to his death in 1922. Satire was Edwards' main mode of expression and he used it sometimes like a rapier to puncture bloated egos and pompous facades and sometimes like a sabre to lay bare the depredations of those who preyed upon the defenceless. His blazing anger was directed at any manifestation of personal or institutional arrogance. The following quotation reveals both the Edwards style and a favourite target:

COME TO CALGARY, the Aquarium City. Full of sharks! Boozorium Park! Seize your opportunity! Do not delay! Come early and avoid the future residential district of Calgary, beautifully situated in the midst of the unparalleled scenic beauties of the bald headed prairie, on a site famed for its badger and gopher holes and renowned in song and story for its entire absence of water. A pleasant place for a murder. Rural mail service promised before the turn of the century.[62]

Edwards' "Society Notes" were exquisite examples of satire in a personal vein. Although supposedly fictitious, many of the "Notes" contained thinly veiled references to local high-society figures, designed to delight most readers and embarrass a few:

Mr. and Mrs. Harry Brinkley have returned from their trip to England where they went on their honeymoon. Mr. Brinkley looks as if he had come through a threshing machine but reports a good time. . . . During his stay in London Mr. Brinkley attended a function at the court being driven home in a patrol wagon.[63]

Edwards was a champion of the underdog. He defended prostitutes and lashed out at moralizing churchmen. He called hospitals places for "sick rich people" and lamented the alarming rate of infant mortality among the poor.[64] Many poor bewildered souls found a friend in Edwards, while other Calgarians feared that he might choose to unmask their questionable actions. Edwards was a complex figure. Popularly labelled a humourist, he had a very serious view of life. A shy man, he had many acquaintances, a fair share of enemies and few close friends. He sought solace from the bottle, yet above all others he despised the distillers as the lowest form of humanity. Indeed, Edwards' championing of the prohibition cause probably did much to

Early members of the Victorian Order of Nurses in Calgary, c. 1912.

A Victorian Order of Nurses baby clinic in Calgary, c. 1912.

ensure its success in Calgary in the 1915 plebscite. Although he mocked pretentious individuals, Edwards' major attacks were on institutions. He believed that society's ills stemmed from outmoded institutions which should be reshaped along the lines of general consensus, taking into account present and future needs. Very much an idealist, Edwards represented the inarticulated aspirations of the urban majority, and through his *Eye Opener* he brought the Calgary example to over 30,000 readers across Canada.

Both Edwards and the other social reformers found plenty to inspire their efforts in Calgary. Squalor and poverty sharply contrasted scenes of commercial prosperity and individual affluence. Overcrowded conditions and high rents forced many to live in dismal surroundings. The infant mortality rate was distressingly high among children of poor families. Although the city boasted a splendid hospital, many could not afford its services. The sight of someone picking over offal in back lanes was not uncommon, and derelicts and drunks endured brutal exposure on Calgary's winter streets. To a degree, there was still an ethnic connotation to social deprivation in Calgary. Poorest were the newly arrived immigrants, particularly those of European origin.

The pre-war depression braked Calgary's internal economic growth, intensified the reforming zeal and gave impetus to those seeking to influence civic policy-making. The voices of organized labour and women became more strident. Social reform held greater sway in church policies, while Bob Edwards launched his devastating barrage at the liquor men. In the light of social and economic trends observable by 1914, Calgary's urban development had reached a transitional stage, with the profound implications of World War I yet to come.

Chapter Three

The Years of Consolidation 1915-1947

Although this period marked no great transformation in Calgary's economy or commercial life, it was characterized by three definite trends. First, there was the instability of commercial grain farming, which, combined with the uncertainty of beef cattle raising, underscored Calgary's economic vulnerability. Secondly, there was an increasing control of local commerce by outside interests. Although a factor during the boom period, this trend was greatly reinforced during these years. The third trend involved the entry of the oil and gas industry into Calgary's commercial life. While the full impact of the new industry would not be felt until a later period, these pioneer years were of crucial importance to Calgary.

ECONOMIC GROWTH AND METROPOLITAN DEVELOPMENT

The outbreak of World War I intensified the demand for western Canadian foodstuffs. Agricultural production increased rapidly, as more land was fenced and turned to commercial grain farming. A bumper wheat crop of 360 million bushels was harvested in 1915, and by 1917 the price of wheat had reached $2.90 a bushel.[1] After the war, production and prices levelled off, and the next 25 years were characterized by wide fluctuations in grain and beef production. Statistics reveal the inconsistent and unprofitable nature of agricultural production after 1920. The value of field crops in Alberta was $142.26 million in 1920, $157.22 million in 1925, $77.31 million in 1935 and, by 1942, $142.14.[2] In spite of improvements in agriculture, the 1915 per acre wheat yield had not been matched by 1945. Western Canada's hard spring wheat had little appeal in the emerging Oriental market, and local milling concerns found it difficult to compete with their rivals in Puget Sound, Washington.

The Depression devastated prairie agriculture. Prices for Number One Northern dropped to 39.375 cents per bushel in 1932. From a yield of 11.5 bushels per acre in 1929, southern Alberta wheat plunged to fewer than three bushels per acre in 1937. Words painted on a farm wagon in 1938 tell the grim tale of prairie agriculture during the Depression:

1929	Dried out
1930	Frozen out
1931	Dried out
1932	Hailed out
1933	Grasshoppered out
1934	Dried out
1935	Rusted out
1936	Dried out
1937	Blown out
1938	Moving out[3]

Although harvests were more promising in the early 1940s, wartime demand for wheat was poor, and prices remained low until the war ended.

Despite Calgary's strong position as a livestock centre during this period, the cattle industry was not able to maintain a consistent rate of growth. Outside markets to absorb an annual surplus of at least 250,000 head were essential to the industry's survival. Ocean freight charges, exchange rates and tariff structures were crucial variables over which Canadian cattlemen had no control. Indeed, the United States tariff was revised three times during this period, with profound implications for the movement of Canadian cattle. The inconsistent markets in Great Britain and the United States resulted in wide fluctuations in exports of cattle and beef, as well as a continuing disequilibrium between live cattle and dressed meat trade.[4]

The nature of the livestock industry was changing. More cattle were sold off farms. This meant a weakening of southern Alberta's pre-eminent position. In 1940, southern Alberta provided less than half the province's 1.3 million cattle; the heaviest concentration was 165,870 head in the parkland belt around Red Deer. The construction of Canada Packers' million-dollar plant in Edmonton undermined Calgary's dominance as Alberta's meat-packing centre. More stringent lease conditions and rising labour costs also cut into the cattleman's profit margins. The difficulty of forecasting long range trends in the industry induced banks to follow conservative lending policies. Bankers valued cattle well below their market value before granting loans against them.[5] Most ranchers carried a high rate of indebtedness into the 1930s, which, combined with the Depression and the closing of the American market, resulted in a period of rapid decline. Many small operators were forced out of business. Before the wartime demand for beef revived the cattle industry, Alberta cattlemen seemed to face a bleak future.[6]

This period marked the centralization of the meat-packing industry. When the external markets were closed to live cattle, meat-packing enterprises were forced to absorb the surplus production. In order to meet increased demands and ensure survival, meat packers became larger and more diversified. Mergers and take-overs were common, and by 1933 Canada Packers and Swift Canada controlled 85 per cent of the meat-packing business.[7] The companies' eastern Canadian headquarters exercised buying control, with the result that Toronto became the leading cattle market in Canada.

Calgary had reflected the economic adjustments associated with the open range industry prior to 1914. Now the city mirrored the subsequent failure of the restructured cattle industry to sustain steady growth. There were too many variables and too much dependence on external markets to handle surplus production. By the 1930s, it was clear that Alberta's best opportunities for success in the cattle industry lay in exporting live cattle to out-of-province markets. Although Calgary remained a livestock centre, both in terms of cattle shipments and packing facilities, there was

little evidence of economic advantage afforded to the city by the cattle industry. However, Calgary did maintain its historic role as spokesman for western livestock interests. In 1938, the Calgary-based *Canadian Cattlemen* began publication. Emphasizing the need for drastic revisions in the cattle industry, this journal provided a forum for western Canadian cattlemen to present their views and unify their case for reform.

In this period, hinterland development regulated economic conditions in Calgary. The city's modest, even erratic growth mirrored patterns in the agricultural and livestock industries. Annual reports of the Board of Trade indicated the dependence of local business on crop conditions. High yields during World War I stimulated business activity. After the 1915 bumper crop, Calgary seemed to have reached economic maturity. Records were set in bank clearances; out-of-town trade increased by 50 per cent; a Boston survey rated Calgary one of the most prosperous cities in North America. In 1921, however, the Board of Trade warned of the sorry state of the retail trade in the city and referred to low grain prices and the unsatisfactory state of the livestock market. The years 1928-29 were the best in Calgary since the war; new industries arrived and construction increased. According to the Board of Trade, this prosperity was due to good wheat crops and to an increase in the American demand for beef. But the Depression showed clearly the effects of rural decline on surrounding urban centres. Plummeting business statistics, bankruptcies and unemployment were urban effects of crop failures and falling grain and cattle prices. The influx into Calgary of rural dwellers seeking employment and relief was an extreme manifestation of a recurring problem.

The close association between Calgary and its hinterland was consolidated in other ways. Calgary remained the headquarters of various agricultural organizations and grain companies as well as the Coal Operators. In 1924, local businessmen persuaded the British milling firm of Spillers Ltd. to erect extensive facilities in Calgary. In 1933, Calgary featured the only oatmeal processing plant in Alberta. The Board of Trade continued to hold seed competitions and tried to protect the local sugar beet industry by lobbying for duties on imported sugar. Changes in the nature of the cattle industry led to increasing numbers of mixed farm operations and small ranchers. Fairly stable prices for cattle in the

Hauling grain to Vulcan elevators, 1928. Prairie agriculture suffered in the inter-war years, affecting the economy of regional centres such as Calgary.

1920s put Pat Burns' meat-packing operations on firm ground, and his reputation for honesty earned him the confidence of small operators.

With greater equalization of freight rates, Winnipeg's advantage in the wholesale trade declined, and Calgary's role as a distributing centre increased. By 1930, the city counted over 200 wholesale houses. Improved roads made Calgary more accessible to rural residents, with the result that the city's retail trade broadened in the 1920s. The growing popularity of the automobile also enhanced Calgary's regional importance. The largest car dealerships in Alberta were located in Calgary, and in 1926 Macklin Ford sold 1,112 cars. The advent of commercial radio emphasized Calgary's growing influence. Local firms advertised sales and products via radio to all parts of southern and south-central Alberta.

There was also a measure of metropolitan consolidation during this period. The Mackenzie Basin Fisheries Ltd. was organized in 1921 and built a cannery and salting plant on the north shore of Lake Athabaska. Henry Marshall Jenkins expanded his retail grocery business to a national scale. In 1918, he operated Canada's first self-serve food store. Ten years later, he owned 17 retail grocery stores throughout western Canada. Jenkins Groceteria Ltd. continued to expand during the Depression, and by the late 1940s included over 40 retail stores, a wholesale grocery business and bakery and candy companies.[8] In 1936, Fred Mannix formed a company and began a career in heavy construction which would make him known across the country. The formation of heavy construction companies in the 1940s signalled the first steps towards greater diversification of the economic base in Calgary.

By the usual yardsticks, Calgary's internal economic growth between 1915 and 1940 stood in sharp contrast to that of the boom period. The highest number of building permits issued in any one year of this period was about half those for 1912 (Appendix, Table XI). Bank clearances provided a reliable gauge to retail sales. The 1941 figure ($343 million) was actually less than in 1921. Falling commercial rents were typical in the 1920s, and retail space exceeded demand. The real estate men were quiet, and many had disappeared from the scene. Figures for Toole, Peet and Company, Calgary's largest real estate firm, show that net income was

erratic and topped $5,000 only four times between 1919 and 1936. Except for a brief period in the late 1920s, activity in the construction industry was sluggish. Only in 1942, with a population influx attracted by Calgary's role in World War II, did the construction industry begin to resemble the vital force of the pre-1914 era.

The presence of the railway continued to be a stable force in Calgary's economy. And so the decision by the CPR in 1931 to close the Ogden shops and lay off 800 men represented the very nadir of the Depression for Calgary. In 1929, the railway companies gave direct employment to about 15 per cent of the labour force and contributed $6.5 million in wages alone to the local economy. In 1941, the main locomotive shop at Ogden was converted by the Canadian government into a munitions factory. At its peak employment, the munitions and railway repair shops gave employment to about 2,500 men. Between 1941 and 1945, the wheel and tender shop was almost doubled in size and three extra railway buildings were added.[9]

During this period, much of Calgary's manufacturing involved production of bulky iron and steel items. In 1929, Manitoba Rolling Mills established a plant, and the Dominion Bridge Company, which had purchased land in Calgary in 1912, finally came to the city. The 1931 census reported that over half of Calgary's manufacturing labour force produced iron and steel items, primarily for a regional market.

As Calgary consolidated its regional position in areas formerly dominated by Winnipeg, various brokerage houses and insurance, trust and investment companies made Calgary their provincial headquarters. In 1929, the T. Eaton Company built a million-dollar store on the corner of Third Street West and Eighth Avenue. In the same year, the Hudson's Bay Company demolished the historic Alexander Block to make way for its new emporium. These new enterprises in Calgary meant that local men no longer wielded major control over the economic development of the city.

Local businessmen found it difficult to attract the investment capital they needed to sustain their entrepreneurial efforts. In 1920, D. E. Black and Company, one of Calgary's most prestigious jewellers, was taken over by Henry Birks and Sons. Alberta Flour Mills was formed in 1915 by local businessmen to help enhance the city's position as a milling centre. By 1923, the plant

Irrigation was crucial to prairie agriculture. These men are working in the 1920s along irrigation dikes on the Sutherland farm in the Calgary area.

Dredging for gravel in the 1920s.

was only partially erected and the company was being kept afloat with loans from affluent stockholders George Lane and William Pearce, who together advanced the company $95,000. But their efforts were in vain. After a spirited promotional campaign by its stockholders, the Alberta Flour Mills Company sold its assets to a less than eager Spillers Ltd. of England. The Calgary Petroleum Products Company, incorporated and backed financially by local interests, made the first significant oil strike at Turner Valley in 1914. Six years later the company faced liquidation, having failed in its intensive efforts to attract outside capital for further development. In 1921, Calgary Petroleum Products Company was bailed out by Imperial Oil Company Ltd., which formed Royalite Oil Company Ltd. to take over the assets and liabilities of the Calgary company. Shareholders of Calgary Petroleum gladly exchanged $116.25 worth of their shares for each $25 share in Royalite.

This infusion of outside capital was a major concern in Calgary. The Board of Trade noted in 1931 that the branch houses of eastern concerns failed to patronize local industry. Smaller establishments could not compete with big department stores and the mail order business. Many folded, while some could not repay the mortgage loans granted on their properties by the city. The most devastating blow came in 1928, when P. Burns and Company sold its meat-packing interests to Dominion Securities Corporation of Toronto for $15 million. The president of the Calgary Board of Trade offered the following epitaph on local commercial autonomy:

> . . . local industries, after being started, fostered and made successful by resident businessmen, are passing into the hands of outside capitalists. The latter, I am afraid, are not likely to have the same interests in our development and in our local institutions as our local citizens.[10]

The flow of outside capital into the city was arrested abruptly by the Depression, and until the crude oil discovery of 1936, there was little to stimulate the local economy. However, the businessmen who managed to survive with limited inventories and small profit margins and the ambitious newcomers who began businesses on shoestring budgets were able to take advantage of the economic upswing accelerated by World War II. Many small businessmen were able to secure choice commercial sites or expand their premises cheaply when city council sold land at greatly reduced values in 1942.

The discovery of oil at Turner Valley in 1914 heralded a new era for Calgary. Though the yield of "black gold" from Turner Valley wells was modest, especially before 1936, it was enough to establish Calgary as an oil and gas centre. When the 1947 discoveries at Leduc Woodbend ushered in Canada's real petroleum era, Calgary was already the national oil capital. During this pioneer period, the degree of involvement by Calgary oilmen and the uncertainty of the Turner Valley deposits had profound effects on the city. In the first place, Calgary acquired a legacy of resident expertise in the oil business. Some local individuals turned expertise into fortunes when areas they leased became sites of major discoveries. Secondly, Calgary reflected the boom-bust, start-stop pattern which nurtured speculation and undermined steady economic growth. Frantic speculation in oil companies and stocks was a new manifestation of the same mentality which had inflated real estate prices before 1914. Indeed, many former real estate men became oil promoters. Excitement generated by news of impending strikes in the Turner Valley revitalized the frontier buoyancy of a previous era. In a 1927 report, the manager of Spillers Ltd. referred to Calgary as a "newly rich city" and intimated that the expensive tastes of Calgarians made them unique in Alberta. However, there were many disappointments. Companies folded regularly as Turner Valley repeatedly promised more than it delivered.

Calgary men had long been interested in the Sheep Creek area as a source of petroleum, and one report claims that the City of Calgary almost took a lease on the property where the Discovery Well "blew in" on May 14, 1914.[11] The strike was made by the Calgary Petroleum Products Company headed by local residents and backed by Calgary's leading real estate men and investors. The effects of this discovery in Calgary were electrifying; overnight the city was transformed into yet another promoter's paradise. Claude Dingman, son of Archibald W. Dingman, who headed the Petroleum Products Company, had this view of the events:

> Overnight an oil boom started with such force that every

vacant store or office was taken over for immediate organization of companies ready for action. Calgary citizens "boomed" the stocks issued, and the city soon filled with an excited throng, some having legitimate intentions, others ready to "Fly-by-night". Printers came in for a rush of business with an hourly demand for prospectuses detailing beautiful pictures of "Black Gold" for the asking. Thousands of stock certificates were madly written out even into the far hours of the night. The land office almost became the scene of a "Stampede". Outside and inside excited ones jostled for the first position on the line-up of buyers of prospective oil lands. But in the main offices of the new companies, the action was at once wonderful and absurd. The buyers of stock .`. . threw their money over the counter into any handy box or desk and even the sight of large bills overflowing into the waste-baskets did not halt the scramble. Some frenzied ones hadn't time to wait on receipts, but ran off rejoicing into the melee next door for another chance at wealth.[12]

Within days, almost a half million dollars had been withdrawn from the savings accounts of thousands of Calgarians. By October 1914, over 500 oil companies had been incorporated with a total capitalization of $83 million.[13] Two years later, amidst the misery and capital shortage engendered by the war, confidence in oil stocks remained unshaken. The *Herald* attributed the large backlog of unpaid taxes partly to the practice among ratepayers of investing available cash in oil companies.[14]

From 1914 to 1923, only 65,000 barrels of oil were recovered from the few wells producing in Turner Valley. Ten barrels a day was average production, while the record daily output stood at 40. Of 19 wells begun by 1920, only six were completed, and given the "ditch geology" methods of the day, all wells could be described as "wildcats". Costs were high and drilling methods primitive. The average well took two years to complete and cost over $50,000. Companies were hampered by poor roads and delays in the arrival of equipment. Since most drilling and rigging machinery was imported from the United States, a 37 per cent duty added to costs. Management was usually inexperienced and inefficient, while marketing and refining facilities were not equipped to handle even the meagre production of Turner Valley

wells. With outside investors reluctant to finance further development, many companies folded and thousands of stock certificates were discarded to gather dust in forgotten corners of Calgary homes.

Two very significant developments during this decade were to have major implications for Calgary. In 1922, Imperial Oil opened its Calgary refinery to handle the high-quality naphtha gas from Turner Valley. The second development began in 1921 when, under the persuasive powers of R.B. Bennett, Imperial Oil Company Ltd. took over the assets of the floundering Calgary Petroleum Products Company. Its subsidiary, Royalite Company Ltd., drilled the famous well that opened up the vast reserves of wet gas known as the Mississippian. In October 1924, the chief driller at the well site of Royalite No. 4 drilled beyond his instructed depth and hit a layer of limestone and gas. The gas was immediately ignited, belching flames high into the air. For years, the dullish red glow in the night sky symbolized to Calgarians the presence of the oil industry, Hell's Half Acre.[15]

The opening of this new production zone by Royalite No. 4 once again enhanced the potential of Turner Valley as a major field. Over the next 10 years, Royalite No. 4 earned a reputation as North America's "wonder well". Daily production averaged 400 barrels, with a gas flow of 20 million c.f.d. Exploratory activity picked up, and the opening of new wells led to wild trading scenes reminiscent of 1914. Speculation and fraud were rife. In 1929, one of Calgary's two stock exchanges traded 200,000 shares daily. Seats on the exchange, which had been $200 in 1926, shot up to $4,000.[16] Oil supply and drilling companies made Calgary their headquarters, and local businessmen experienced a steady demand for foodstuffs, clothing, construction materials and other supplies. Approximately 200 oil and related companies were in the city by 1930.[17]

Yet in spite of increased exploration and speculative activity, the necessary outside investment capital was not attracted to Turner Valley. Fiscal agents for local companies spent a great deal of time in Great Britain trying unsuccessfully to interest British capitalists in the future of Turner Valley. As a result, a high percentage of the working capital was supplied by the operators themselves, most of whom were Calgary residents.[18] In all probability, the gloomy outlook at the end of 1929 was exacerbated by

CPR Locomotive No. 5152 being overhauled at the Ogden Shops. The Ogden facilities were a major employer in the city, and the decision by the CPR to lay off 800 men in 1931 represented the nadir of the Depression in Calgary.

Oil drillers at Dingman No. 1, May 1914. The discovery of oil at this well in the Turner Valley, about 30 miles southwest of Calgary, marked the birth of western Canada's petroleum industry. For more than 30 years, until the Leduc discovery after World War II, the Turner Valley field was Canada's major oil producer.

Oil fever brought hundreds of new companies into being overnight.

The discovery of oil in 1914 led to frantic speculation, a new manifestation of the 1911-12 real estate fever. During the brief but spectacular oil boom, ordinary business came to a standstill and tens of thousands of dollars changed hands daily. Though the Turner Valley discovery was of profound long-term significance to Calgary, it did not prove to be the immediate bonanza that Calgarians had anticipated.

A New Valley oil well, one of hundreds drilled after 1914.

a growing belief that Turner Valley held only wet gas and salt water. By the time the Depression hit western Canada, drilling rates had slowed appreciably, and many had lost faith in their chances of finding the pools of crude oil.

However, it was through the energy and initiative of Calgary men that crude oil was finally discovered in 1936. Robert A. Brown Sr., the superintendent of Calgary's street railway system and a long-time observer of the oil scene, was convinced that there was crude oil in the west flank of Turner Valley. Since no geologist would agree with him, he could find no company to test his theory. In the early 1930s, Brown formed Turner Valley Royalties, and with financial backing from publisher George Bell and lawyer Jack Moyer, he raised sufficient funds to begin drilling in 1934. Brown mortgaged his house, sold his car and borrowed heavily on his insurance policies to keep the company operating. In June 1936, at a depth of 6,800 feet, his perseverance and confidence paid off. Turner Valley Royalties No. 1 "blew in". The well was Canada's first real evidence of petroleum wealth, and total production from Turner Valley soared to 2 million barrels in 1937.

The oil industry began to stabilize after 1936, and new prosperity in Calgary confirmed its position as the nation's oil capital. Calgary became an administrative centre in 1938 when the Alberta government established the Oil and Natural Gas Conservation Board in the city. In 1939, the British-American Oil Company built the city's second oil refinery. Demand for Turner Valley crude intensified in the wake of worsening international relations. Seventy-six wells were producing by 1939. The value of total production topped $11 million in 1938, and by the same year the original $25 Royalite share had earned over $12,000. World War II further stimulated production, which peaked at 9.7 million barrels in 1942. Yet by 1945, Turner Valley was already a declining field. On February 14, 1947, Imperial Oil's Leduc No. 1 "blew in", and with it Alberta's oil and gas industry was redefined on an unprecedented scale. The post-war oil boom was underway and Calgary began a period of phenomenal urban growth as the centre of a burgeoning industry.

POPULATION GROWTH AND ETHNIC RELATIONSHIPS

The period between 1916 and 1941 is unique in Calgary's history, for only during these years did population growth reflect natural increase rather than immigration. Between 1916 and 1941, Calgary's population grew by 32,390 to a total of 88,904 (Appendix, Table IV). Fewer than 9,000 of this figure represented migration into the city. In fact, 7,000 people actually left Calgary in the 1930s. In 1911, the Calgary birthrate was 30.1 per thousand, substantially higher than the provincial rate of 23.6. When the city's birthrate peaked at 36.6 in 1921, it was far ahead of Alberta's 28.2. Even during the Depression, Calgary's birthrate hovered around the 21.0 mark. The population remained quite young by modern standards. Only 2.3 per cent of the population was over 64 in 1921, as compared with 9.3 per cent 30 years later (Appendix, Table IX).[19]

Although precise figures are not available, Calgary's faster growth rate compared to surrounding areas indicates that the urban drift had begun by the 1920s. The combined populations of Airdrie, Carstairs, Cayley, Cochrane, Coleman, Didsbury, High River and Okotoks increased by only 1,469, or 34 per cent, between 1916 and 1946. Calgary's increase was over 77 per cent. During the Depression, many people from smaller centres came to Calgary hoping to take advantage of the city's expanded relief services. Figures suggest that most of these new arrivals stayed. The outbreak of World War II intensified migration to Calgary from other centres. Between 1941 and 1946, 3,361 families arrived in Calgary from other points in Alberta. About half of this number came from farms. During the same years, 2,507 families came from other provinces, with former farm dwellers accounting for 16.2 per cent.[20]

The Anglo-Saxon character of Calgary's population became entrenched during this period. Of a total population of 83,761 in 1931, over 70,000 were of British origin. A scant 7,225 had been born in Europe, and all ethnic groups except the Chinese accounted for a good proportion of the Canadian-born. In 1941, 86.5 per cent of Calgary's population listed English as their mother tongue, and by 1946 the city's Canadian-born population had risen to 69 per cent from 55 per cent in 1931 (Appendix, Tables V, VI, VII). In spite of the pressures to assimilate, ethnic groups continued to retain parts of their cultural heritage. Compared to Edmonton, Calgary received numerically more Scandinavians, Russians, Hungarians and Italians. Except for the

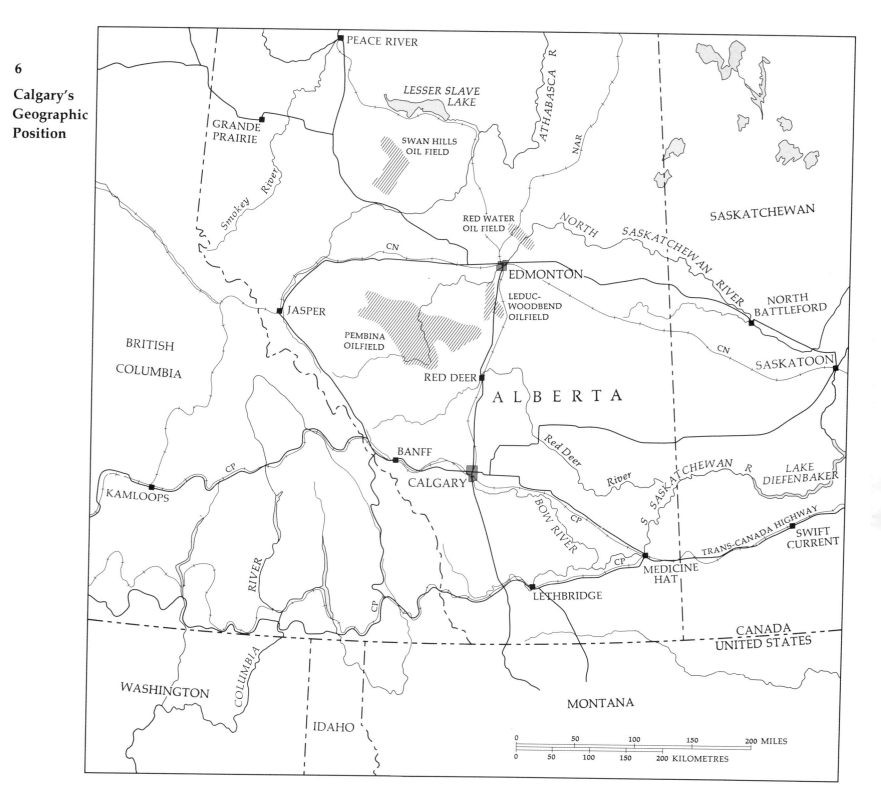

6

Calgary's Geographic Position

PEACE RIVER

GRANDE PRAIRIE

Smokey River

LESSER SLAVE LAKE

SWAN HILLS OIL FIELD

ATHABASCA R

NAR

SASKATCHEWAN

RED WATER OIL FIELD

NORTH

SASKATCHEWAN RIVER

CN

EDMONTON

BRITISH

COLUMBIA

JASPER

LEDUC-WOODBEND OILFIELD

PEMBINA OILFIELD

NORTH BATTLEFORD

CN

SASKATOON

RED DEER

A L B E R T A

Red Deer

BANFF

River

CP

LAKE DIEFENBAKER

KAMLOOPS

CALGARY

BOW RIVER

CP

S SASKATCHEWAN R

CP

TRANS-CANADA HIGHWAY

SWIFT CURRENT

COLUMBIA

RIVER

CP

MEDICINE HAT

LETHBRIDGE

CANADA

UNITED STATES

WASHINGTON

MONTANA

IDAHO

0	50	100	150	200 MILES

0	50	100	150	200 KILOMETRES

Chinese, the ratio of men to women was fairly equal, indicating that whole families were migrating (Appendix, Table II). Social customs were preserved in the privacy of homes and small social gatherings. But in public life, Anglo-Saxon dominance was unchallenged.

A few European immigrants had begun to achieve success in business by this time. Peter Brasso arrived in Calgary from Denmark in 1929. He started his own business in 1930 and by 1946 operated one of the city's more successful used car dealerships and owned the Brasso Fur Farms in Bowness. Niels Weismose came to Calgary in 1927, also from Denmark. After taking a night course in English, he began his furniture business with $48 cash. By 1948, he operated one of Calgary's most successful furniture stores.[21]

However, the World Wars and the Depression served to heighten racial tensions. Antagonism towards German residents flared up in 1916, when mobs of soldiers and civilians wrecked the White Lunch Restaurant and demolished portions of the Riverside Hotel. It was city council policy between 1916-18 to employ only British subjects and to dismiss all individuals born in alien territory. Thus, it is not surprising that only 876 people gave Germany as their place of origin in the census of 1921. In 1942, men of German origin who were not volunteering for active service were targets of public anger. After the conscription referendum in 1942, one irate resident insisted that pro-German sentiment had led the Bridgeland community to vote against conscription.[22] People of Japanese background were not encouraged to live in Calgary during World War II, and in 1942, city council voiced opposition to allowing Japanese businessmen from Vancouver to establish themselves in Calgary.[23]

In these years, there was little change in the basic structure of Calgary's labour force, which showed a total increase of approximately 7,000 between 1911-31, of which more than half occurred in 1921-31. Most were employed in the service and trade categories, which in 1921 accounted for about 50 per cent of the labour force. Ten years later, over 60 per cent of Calgary workers were employed as clerks or in industries associated with service or trade, as compared with approximately 15 per cent in manufacturing.[24]

By stimulating Calgary's economy in the construction industry and wartime services, World War II contributed to a higher standard of living as well as to a widening of the socio-economic brackets. Calgary's average family income in 1946 was $2,122, $214 above the provincial average. One-sixth of the work force earned over $4,950, compared with a provincial figure of one-twelfth and one-eighth in Edmonton. Calgary had 2,500 fewer dwellings than Edmonton, but had 144 more houses worth over $10,000. However, substantially fewer individuals owned homes in Calgary than in Edmonton.[25] The high rate of transience during the war years was certainly a factor in this statistic, but the trend had been in evidence at the outbreak of the war.

The increasing degree of union protection and improved working conditions, wages and benefits resulted in greater opportunities for working class people to pursue a more individual lifestyle. Particularly in the 1920s, advancements such as the 48-hour week, greater job security, group insurance schemes and pension plans affected a large proportion of the labour force. Working class families also made advances in areas of public health and education when free baby clinics and school textbooks were provided in the 1920s. Some employers felt they had lost control over their employees and bemoaned work time lost through idleness and absences. Some blamed social diversions like the Alberta Football Coupon Competition and the 110 slot machines operating in Calgary in 1924. Other employers offered bonuses to dissuade their workers from accepting the 48-hour week. In 1925, a spokesman for a leading manufacturing company in Calgary maintained that regardless of the powers of labour, his company would continue to hire and fire at will.

The Depression brought a halt to the progress of the working class towards social and economic parity, but it was also a time which produced an enduring change in public attitude towards the social responsibility of government. In 1925, Calgary council had stated: " . . . this city does not recognize that it owes any citizen a living; if any relief is extended, it will be not as a right but on compassionate grounds."[26] But during the Depression, local governments accepted responsibility for social welfare on an unprecedented scale, and many publicly funded bodies extended material assistance to the needy.

The establishment of the CPR railway shops at Ogden also altered the personality of organized labour in the city. During

In the heart of "Sandstone City". This 1915 view, taken from the Alberta Hotel, shows the north side of Eighth Avenue. Construction in Calgary came to a virtual standstill during and immediately after World War I.

World War I, the rise of the guild-oriented building trades was challenged by the more militant railway workers, particularly the machinists. This resulted in a permanent divisiveness within the local Trades and Labour Council that had widespread political ramifications, for labour found it difficult to speak with a single voice on civic issues or to support any one candidate for office. Thus it could be argued that the extension of labour activity in Calgary to include the railway workers tended to polarize rather than fuse the local labour movement.

After an unsuccessful display of union solidarity during the freighthandlers' strike of 1918, a divided Trades and Labour Council rejected the One Big Union Movement and subsequently turned its back on militantism by failing to support the Winnipeg General Strike in 1919. By 1920, moderation and a firm belief in conciliation marked the official attitude of organized labour in Calgary. Even during the Depression, the attitudes of most unions remained non-militant. There was no sustained protest from organized labour when wage reductions were effected by conciliation boards. Job security was rarely jeopardized by strikes, and wages in the city remained the highest in the province.

During World War I, women achieved many major goals. Prohibition came in 1915, and the Dominion franchise followed at the end of the war. Women entered the labour force in increasing numbers and began to fill elected positions in municipal politics. The return of large numbers of men after the war did not result in a complete reversion to pre-war labour patterns. While women continued as dynamic forces in social reform, they also maintained their position as an integral part of the work force. In the early 1920s, a Women's Labour League was formed. This organization was particularly active in drawing attention to the plight of the aged in the city. By 1931, half of Calgary's social welfare positions were held by women.

THE URBAN LANDSCAPE

After the collapse of the pre-World War I building boom, Calgary experienced virtually no physical expansion until a chronic housing shortage during World War II again stimulated activity in the construction industry. Later city councils not only inherited the results of pre-1914 extravagances, but also had to implement policies in a more austere economic environment. Calgary's physical growth during this period involved policy reactions and modifications in an area which had been delineated by 1912.

Manufacturing land use did not change during this period since the city's industrial policy of 1911 had allowed for ample expansion. Most incoming industries were located in Manchester or in the adjoining manufacturing sites along the Macleod Trail. The city had also set aside acreage in the Nose Creek area for future industrial parks. Refining facilities were built in east Calgary, consolidating the manufacturing character of the southeast corridor between the stockyards and the Ogden repair shops.

In terms of commercial development, the most observable trend was the continued domination of the downtown core. This was facilitated by excellent streetcar service. Also, Calgary's slow growth after 1912 brought an end to the spiralling demand for rental space. Finally, there were municipal government policies that appeared unsympathetic to expanding commercial land use.

Most streetcar routes entered the downtown area, and the corner of Eighth Avenue and First Street West, where the streetcars converged, became the centre of retail activity. Fares were very reasonable and were actually reduced in the early 1920s. In the good commercial year of 1929, approximately one-third of the population used the streetcars daily.[27] In 1944, that percentage was maintained when over 67,000 passengers used public transportation each day. Although the automobile was increasing in popularity, it had not begun to divert commercial activity from the main business centre.

Slow economic growth after 1912 also contributed to the continuing dominance of the downtown business area. Although some retailers moved out of the downtown district to take advantage of lower rentals, the post-World War I period saw a virtual stagnation in building development. Falling land prices led to a stabilization of rents, which meant that small businessmen could retain their downtown locations. During the Depression, landlords actually competed with each other to secure business tenants. Only in the premium areas along Eighth Avenue were rents comparatively high. Rent on the tiny Eighth Avenue Nut House was more than double that paid by larger confectionery stores on First Street West or in the Roxborough Block on 26th Avenue

Throughout the 1930s and early 1940s, Calgary experienced a severe housing shortage. This aerial view of Calgary in the 1940s shows a large housing project in the Hillhurst district.

South. In the early 1940s, rental space along busy Ninth and Eleventh Avenues was sometimes less than half that along Eighth Avenue. The shortage of business and residential space brought on by the population influx during World War II forced rents up and drove developers to the cheaper land areas well beyond the downtown centre. Only with the subsequent advent of suburban shopping plazas did the central retail district begin to relinquish its commercial dominance.

Civic policy militated against commercial expansion outside the central business area. The imprecise nature of the building bylaw produced conflicts in which the homeowner enjoyed preferential treatment over the businessman. The establishment of commercial enterprises was contingent upon the approval of neighbouring residents. Even when this was obtained, the city reserved the right of disallowance.[28] When commercial expansion was not vigorous, it was fairly easy for homeowners to petition successfully for adjoining blocks to be designated residential. In other areas, commercial expansion was prevented by homeowners who refused to sell. By enjoying lower residential assessment, they could afford to wait until demand for commercial space forced land prices up. Therefore, the cluster of business establishments along the streetcar routes were unable to consolidate themselves or compete with the downtown core.

In the face of stringent financial limitations, councils were obliged to implement policies designed to restrict physical growth. These policies, by encouraging a closer concentration of population, contributed towards multiple land use in the inner city area and depressed land prices in the outer suburbs. One effect of the pre-1914 land boom had been the over-extension of residential districts. Land in many subdivisions had been sold cheaply on the assurance of subsequent amenities like streets and utilities. Consequently, houses were scattered throughout the city virtually isolated from main roads and utility trunk lines. In 1922, a report by a special council committee designated 28 of Calgary's 36 sections as unimproved, while eight years later it was estimated that over 80 per cent of the city's area was unoccupied. In 1946, Calgary had 28,506 occupied dwellings. Thirty per cent had been built before 1911, and only 6,055 were erected between 1921 and 1940.

The continued reversion of land to the city in lieu of unpaid taxes placed additional strains on the limited financial resources of municipal governments. Over $200,000 worth of property accrued to the city in 1914 alone. By the following year, over $4.3 million were owing in taxation arrears, and the trend continued over the years. In 1933, the city took title to 1,600 pieces of property. Nine years later, the value of disposable property owned by the City of Calgary was approximately $5 million[30]

Faced with a scattered population and with land increasingly being removed from the assessment rolls, council initiated a formal policy of growth restriction in 1920. This involved curtailing streetcar services, restricting utilities beyond a designated inner city area and levying high assessments in outlying areas on non-agricultural land. Incentive programs were built into this policy. Owners of lots in surrounding areas were encouraged to exchange them for corresponding pieces of property closer to the city centre. A special house-moving fund was established in 1929 and levied against the city utilities, "for the purpose of encouraging and assisting the moving of buildings from the outer areas into the inner area".[31] A year later, a bylaw was passed prohibiting the sale of property in outlying areas for construction purposes unless adjacent to an existing building.

This policy had several implications for future development. Land prices in outlying areas dropped dramatically. Considerable acreage reverted to agricultural use and was acquired later by developers for very low prices. Council aided in this process during World War II when, in a shortsighted effort to acquire needed revenue and promote housing, it adopted a policy whereby city-owned land was sold at 50 per cent of its assessed value. This figure was later dropped to 25 per cent, and in 1944 each application was judged on its individual merits. Within a few short years, the city had disposed of much of its land holdings for a total of $377,000. A parcel of 1.6 acres in Spruce Cliff was sold for $240. Nineteen acres were sold in Glendale for $500 cash. A.J. Mayland refused to pay $75 an acre for land in present-day Mayland Heights, so the city offered it to him for $30 per acre. Lots in West Hillhurst sold for $20 each, while land in industrial subdivisions went for $40 per lot or less. Prime commercial space was sold cheaply. Macklin Motors bought the northwest corner of Eleventh Avenue and First Street West for approximately 60 per cent of its assessed value. Ten lots on the

7

**Land Use
in Calgary,
1945**

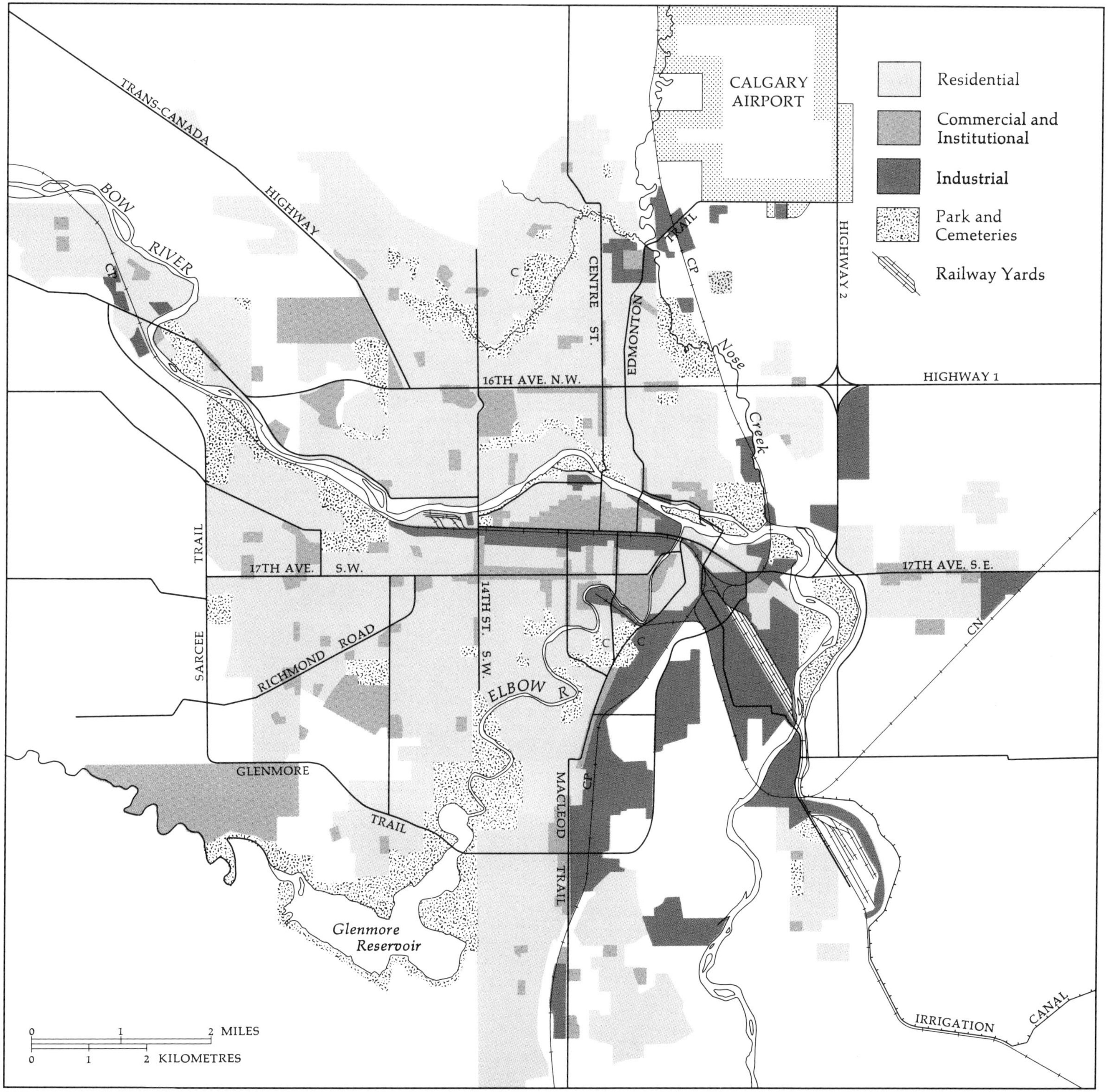

CALGARY
AIRPORT

Residential

Commercial and
Institutional

Industrial

Park and
Cemeteries

Railway Yards

TRANS-CANADA HIGHWAY

BOW RIVER

CP

CENTRE ST.

EDMONTON TRAIL

CP

Nose Creek

HIGHWAY 2

HIGHWAY 1

16TH AVE. N.W.

C

TRAIL

SARCEE

17TH AVE. S.W.

RICHMOND ROAD

14TH ST. S.W.

ELBOW R

C C

17TH AVE. S.E.

CN

GLENMORE

TRAIL

MACLEOD TRAIL

CP

Glenmore
Reservoir

IRRIGATION CANAL

| 0 | | 1 | | 2 MILES |

| 0 | 1 | | 2 KILOMETRES |

The affluent lifestyle of Calgary's wealthy families was often displayed in lavish homes, like the T.J.S. Skinner residence. Skinner was one of the city's prominent real estate dealers.

Entrance hall in the Skinner residence.

The drawing room.

The billiard room.

A downstairs lounge.

corner of Sixteenth Avenue North and Fourteenth Street West went for $1,000 in 1941. By 1945, speculative evils had once more been launched on the city, and in 1946 a city lands committee recommended that the policy of selling city lands cheaply be discontinued.[32]

Calgary's inner area absorbed a population increase of over 100 per cent between 1911 and 1946, and this affected residential land use, particularly in areas contiguous to the business district. Although apartments appeared increasingly in central areas, existing water and sewerage services were insufficient to allow construction of large, high-density units. Instead, large, single family houses were converted into multiple dwelling units. In 1929, an investigation into housing conditions in Calgary revealed that the area between the CPR mainline and Seventeenth Avenue South was the most congested in the city. Fully one-third of the families surveyed lived in one or two rooms sublet in large houses. Inadequate toilet and washing facilities in these dwellings posed potential health hazards.

In addition to contributing to residential congestion, the official restricted-growth policy resulted in multiple land use in the central areas. Indeed, when the zoning bylaw became effective in the early 1930s, it provided for a multiple use district. Containment was virtually impossible, especially in the early 1940s, when an acute housing shortage forced civic authorities to relax regulations. Site area was reduced for duplexes, and approval was easily secured to convert almost any dwelling into suites anywhere in the city. The result was an acceleration of heterogeneous land usage along the streetcar routes and especially near existing business and factory areas (see Map 7).

The policy of restricted growth reaffirmed pre-1914 residential patterns. Adequately serviced by utilities and the street railway and with districts subject to building restrictions, the southwest portion of the city was unchallenged as the most desirable residential area. Mount Royal retained its pre-eminence. Expansion to the north and east was slow and modest. Falling land prices in the 1920s meant lower assessments, which did little to encourage the city to spend money expanding utilities. Only in the 1960s did areas in the northwest and southeast begin to rival the residential supremacy of the southwest.

The emergence of deprived residential districts during this period was not due solely to factors of age or multiple-use zoning as was to be the case in the post-1950 period. In outlying areas, poorer residential districts were those favoured with streetcar routes, but without full utility service or building restrictions. Bowness and Forest Lawn were two such communities. Both were situated outside the city limits but were within Calgary's urban purview. In 1929, large unserviced lots were offered in Bowness for $100 on the guarantee that annual taxes would not exceed $1.00. Residents of Forest Lawn, many of them European immigrants, were within reasonable commuting distance of the east Calgary factories via the street railway that ran to adjoining Albert Park. Bowness was connected directly to Calgary by the street railway and became somewhat of a "shack town" in the 1930s. The governing rural municipalities were unable to regulate growth in these villages despite aid from the Calgary Town Planning Commission in the early 1930s. When the communities of Bowness and Forest Lawn were incorporated into the City of Calgary in the early 1960s, they continued to function as lower-priced residential areas.

Within the city, civic officials appeared unable to control undesirable building trends. Construction often proceeded before the issuance of permits. Some houses violated the building bylaw with respect to placement and quality of building materials. The bylaw itself was specific only on total lot size, with the result that frontages varied greatly. In spite of efforts to encourage wider frontages, housing construction continued on narrow 25-foot lots and resulted in small, closely packed neighbourhoods.

In this period, the role of the street railway and utility extensions in the growth of residential districts was more observable than in the pre-World War I years. The presence of the street railway definitely determined the extent of residential growth and was a key factor in terms of spatial distribution. However, the availability of essential utilities continued to be even more important in the differentiation of districts, and the cheapest houses were in new residential areas where utility extensions lagged considerably behind street railway services. Thus, by controlling utility extensions to limit growth, the civic authorities were contributing to the differentiation of residential districts, a power essentially denied them before the 1930s by the imprecise provisions and limited scope of the building and zoning bylaws.

Zoning played a minor role in determining Calgary's urban landscape during this period. The building bylaw provided for

Calgary in 1947, on the eve of renewed expansion and growth.

Relief marchers in 1935. The United Married Men's Association banner reads "We Stand Behind 12,000 On Relief." These men, like numerous others in Calgary and elsewhere, were protesting inadequate relief measures from all levels of government. But the City of Calgary, already in severe financial straits by 1931, did little about relief except to protest against the insufficient provincial and federal support.

only two types of districts — residential and business. In other areas, it was vague and of dubious legal force. In 1929, the Alberta Town Planning Act empowered cities to appoint town planning commissions whose mandate would include the preparation of a zoning bylaw. Although the new bylaw allowed for four districts instead of two and provided for single family, two family and multiple dwelling districts, it only applied to the inner city area. A companion study was also made of existing transportation routes, and a major street and arterial highway plan was drawn up, designed primarily to relieve traffic congestion in the downtown area. This scheme was shelved during the Depression, and the zoning bylaw was used basically to accommodate the increasing trend towards multiple dwellings. However, both the zoning bylaw and the arterial highway plan recognized two areas of concern which had resulted partly from policies of restricted growth. One was the increasing level of traffic congestion in the downtown area; the other was the presence of an incipient housing shortage.

The zoning bylaw concentrated on multiple dwelling districts, in part, to ease the housing shortage brought on by the prosperity of 1928-29. Considerable demand for small houses with reasonable rent led council to explore ways in which the city could erect municipal houses. The issuance of $2.00 permits in 1930 to allow tent dwellings came after council was advised that a provision for municipal housing was beyond its legal jurisdiction. In the 1930s, the situation worsened and then became intolerable under the pressure of an increasing wartime population. The provincial government's legislated controls on investment capital discouraged mortgage money, and again the city explored the possibilities of cheap municipal housing. Stipulations in the zoning bylaw were relaxed considerably. Landlord Thomas Underwood wrote in 1944: "People are living in places they never dreamt of before and still they keep coming in from different points."[33] Fortunately, wartime housing did become available in Calgary as part of the Dominion government's assistance to cities making substantial contributions to the war effort.

THE URBAN COMMUNITY: SOCIAL AND POLITICAL LIFE

Two main features characterized the further development of local government in Calgary. One concerned the city's ongoing financial problems; the other was labour's involvement in municipal politics. Both brought an increased degree of public responsibility to civic government and ended the long tradition of city councils as agents of growth.

By 1917, it was obvious that the City of Calgary's finances were in a deplorable state.[34] The substantial bonded indebtedness incurred during the boom period necessitated high annual interest payments on debentures, as well as a sizeable contribution to the sinking fund. These payments totalled approximately $1.6 million in 1917. Moreover, the pre-war policy of borrowing against future taxation revenue had proved disastrous. From 1914, arrears in taxation accumulated until by the beginning of 1917 over $3.5 million remained uncollected on the tax rolls. With average annual arrears accounting for about half of the funds needed for expenditures between 1915 and 1917, civic authorities were forced into short-term borrowing. Yet by 1920, the city had over $5 million in uncollected taxes against which a loan of $1.5 million was owing to an American investment house. Payment of other loans on local banks meant that the city's $1 million line of credit for 1921 had been used up before a dollar in taxation revenue had been collected.

Although a combination of high bonded indebtedness and falling taxation revenue was the chief cause of financial distress, there were other factors. The city could not secure a good price for its sinking fund bonds, because the fund itself was in default of $500,000. The council's policy of granting mortgages to local businessmen out of the sinking fund was a terrible mistake. Some had defaulted, and almost all were in arrears with both principal and interest repayments, as well as taxation. Abnormally high assessments were reduced drastically by the court of revision. This action resulted in an increase in the percentage of gross debt as well as a decrease in investor confidence. Mayor Michael Costello wrote in 1918 that the Toronto bond houses were totally lacking in sympathy towards Calgary and were unwilling to help the city in a time of need.

Not surprisingly, the main efforts in municipal government between 1915 and 1925 were directed at the city's financial problems. Tax sales were held, penalties for arrears increased and concessions were granted for early payment of taxes. Water and electricity rates were raised, and additional profits were diverted from the utilities into general revenue. A much higher portion of the general revenue was used for the retirement of debentures. Annual levies to the sinking fund were first suspended and later reduced. New sources of revenue were explored. In 1916, a business tax was introduced that assessed all businesses, trades and professions for a sum equal to the full rental value of their premises. Set originally at six per cent, the tax was increased to ten per cent in the early 1920s and later reduced to eight per cent in more prosperous times towards the end of the decade. In 1921, over the strenuous objection of labour, council approved a service tax involving a direct levy against the income of all ratepayers. Not only was this tax immensely unpopular and difficult to collect, but the local Trades and Labour Council expressed a desire to test its legality in the courts. In 1922, the measure was soundly defeated in a plebiscite, and both the tax and the alderman who had championed it faded into obscurity.

The most effective remedy, however, involved drastic curtailment of both capital and general expenditures. Local improvements were trimmed considerably, and where implemented, the financial burden for improvements fell increasingly on the immediate beneficiaries. Between 1921 and 1928, the street railway department purchased no new vehicles, while apparent inadequacies in the city's water supply went unattended. In 1925-26, a low point was reached, with gross annual municipal expenditures totalling slightly more than $100,000. But there were positive signs. The increasing payment of tax arrears, when added to the annual collectible taxes, meant carry-over surpluses and a falling mill rate.

The impact of the Depression re-emphasized the vulnerable nature of civic finances, which by 1929 were exhibiting signs of rejuvenation. The enormous demands for relief measures led to short-term borrowing and a drastic reshaping of spending priorities. Between 1932 and 1935, the city borrowed $1.3 million from the provincial government alone. Relief payments increased by 1,030 per cent from 1929 to 1934, and social welfare expenditures by 214 per cent. Fixed charges also increased, but spending was down 22 per cent in the planning department, 35 per cent on parks and recreation, 33 per cent in the public works

department and 40 per cent on engineering maintenance. In addition, the total number of civic employees decreased by approximately 25 per cent between 1929 and 1935. In 1935, the mill rate was up to 50 and even at that figure was insufficient to meet the substantial annual interest bill of $1.6 million. This high interest payment caused major concern, and civic officials were frustrated by their lack of power to recall debentures and re-issue them at the lower current interest rates.

At the 1935 conference of Alberta municipalities, Calgary led the way in pressing for more favourable legislation respecting civic powers to renegotiate long-term financing. The result for Calgary was the introduction, in 1937, of the Fortin Refinancing Plan. This plan cancelled City of Calgary bonds in the sinking fund and spread the remaining debt over 25 years. The effect was a reduction of the capital debt by $7 million and an annual saving of over half a million dollars in interest payments. Soon after, the maturation of debentures in all three utilities freed additional funds for general revenue or utility expansion. With the spectre of heavy debt charges banished, the city could once again consider the need for capital expenditures and the taxation revenue necessary to maintain them. The streetcar system was obsolete, and debate raged over the merits of both the gasoline bus and the trackless trolley as replacements. In addition, a new general hospital was needed to replace the woefully inadequate existing facilities.

The precarious nature of Calgary's finances between the wars indicated the inadequacy of the property tax as the dominant source of civic revenue. Exempted property, like the large holdings of the CPR or the enormous tracts of forfeited land within the corporate limits, meant that the major tax burden was borne by resident property holders. While councils did make efforts to explore alternative measures, like the business tax or the abortive service (Hugill) tax, they settled on reducing the financial burden to conscientious taxpayers by collecting and securing loans against tax arrears. This understandable but short-run policy had inevitable ramifications during the Depression, when massive relief demands and greatly diminished tax arrears put the city in a worse position than in the early 1920s. As Mayor Andrew Davison pointed out in 1935, civic governments in the pre-Depression years were able to collect their total annual levy because of arrear

William "Bible Bill" Aberhart, premier of Alberta from 1935 until his death in 1943. This energetic and charismatic school principal used the radio waves and religious fervour to create the Social Credit phenomenon. Aberhart is shown here making a speech at the First Anniversary Picnic on St. George's Island, September 1936.

Social Credit publicity on a hand flatcar at the Ogden Shops, 1935. The Depression brought not only misery and despair, but also numbing bewilderment over a world "gone crazy". William Aberhart's optimistic belief in economic regeneration through a drastic but simple revision of monetary policies proved irresistible. Attracted to the Social Credit Party by utopian solutions, Albertans unequivocally cast in their lot with the golden-tongued Aberhart.

payments, whereas in the 1930s the current annual collections represented about 75 per cent of budgeted revenue. It was mainly for this reason that Calgary pressed higher levels of government to assume total responsibility for municipal relief. Furthermore, by maintaining that the city's present tax structure was confiscatory, civic officials felt justified in requesting a fair share of provincial levies, particularly regarding liquor taxes. In a general sense, Calgary's financial quagmire was part of a national problem which resulted in the historic Rowell Sirois Royal Commission on Dominion-Provincial Relations.

This period marked the entry of labour representatives into local government. Between 1915 and 1920, various amendments to the city charter extended the franchise to all residents without distinction other than length of residence in the city. Property qualifications for the positions of mayor, commissioner and alderman were gradually eliminated. Proportional voting was introduced in 1917, and provision was made for the implementation of the Populist doctrine of "Initiative, Referendum and Recall". By the end of World War I, municipal office had ceased to be the right of property, and the era of the Labour alderman had begun.

The most significant development in municipal politics after 1918 was the election of candidates on a quasi-party basis. The Citizens' Committee, or Civic Government Association, nominated candidates, usually from the business community, and was a strong force during this period, supporting the successful mayoralty candidate throughout the 1920s. The Civic Government Association opposed payment to aldermen, advocated the personal taxation of private citizens and called for cost-saving wherever possible. Except for a period in the early 1920s when it appeared as if Labour might rise to power, the CGA, as it came to be known, nominated most of the successful candidates for civic office.

Opposed to the CGA were the Labour candidates who were nominated under the auspices of the Dominion Labour Party and supported by the various trade unions. Labour's share of the popular vote increased after 1918, rising steadily from 20 to 30 per cent between 1918 and 1920. By 1921, Labour was clearly a force, and it was the dominant group in council by 1922. Labour aldermen stressed the maintenance and extension of municipal ser-

vices without extra cost to the taxpayer. They advocated a hardline approach to monopolies such as the gas company and tended to guard the interests of the employee, specifically the civic worker. Labour's hopes of controlling civic government declined after 1922, but there were always enough Labour aldermen on council to provide an opposing block to CGA candidates.

Support for these two groups was shown in the voting patterns. Generally, Labour drew votes from north Calgary and the southeast. The CGA was strongest in the southwest and the west. The Labour vote was always considered far smaller than union strength would indicate. In fact, Calgary civic voting patterns demonstrated an enduring catholicity. In many elections, it was impossible to differentiate districts or class interests on the basis of voting preferences. The abolition of the ward system in 1913 also affected Labour's election chances by dissipating the potential of a Labour bloc vote and by contributing to the dominance of individual appeal over issues at the polls. Despite these factors, the popularity of the CGA during the Depression does seem surprising. But since these were the years of communist and extreme socialist doctrine, the tax-paying voters were apparently more influenced by the CGA promises to cut expenditures than by the radicals' rhetoric of misery. The Labour vote was fractured further by Communist and Socialist Party candidates running for civic offices. But the first avowed Communist was not elected until 1938, when the worst of the Depression was over.

Despite major involvement in municipal government, neither the CGA nor the Labour group functioned as a political party, although the Labour group was interested in bringing the machinery of party politics to local government. While it is true that some issues polarized the rival groups, the discipline of formal political parties was absent. Neither group was united by leadership, and beyond the articulation of general grievances, there were few well-defined priorities. The CGA nominated candidates put forward by private organizations like Rotary or Kiwanis, while Labour candidates were endorsed by different trade union groups in the city. Furthermore, the ability of one group to wield authority by virtue of numerical strength was limited. There were always independent aldermen, and aspiring council mavericks conducted campaigns based mainly on asser-

The first Calgary Stampede opened in 1912, but World War I delayed the second event until 1919, when a "Victory Stampede" was held. The Stampede then became an annual event, absorbing the old Calgary Exhibition in 1923 and offering a winning combination of rodeo excitement and the agricultural industry of southern Alberta.

Diving horse act, 1919.
Horse and rider dived 50
feet into 10-foot tank of
water.

A street event at the 1926 Stampede.

The Calgary Brewery buffalo team in the Victoria Park arena, 1925.

Part of the wild horse race
at the 1924 Stampede.

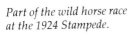

tions of independence from either Labour or the CGA.

Calgary civic government displayed a more striking resemblance to the popular ideal of group government than to the classic concept of party politics. Ostensibly, the United Farmers of Alberta were committed to this ideal, and the theoretical merits of government by balanced groups were widely paraded in Calgary, often by the compelling figure of Henry Wise Wood himself, the farmer-philosopher leader of the UFA.[35] It was hardly surprising to find candidates for civic office nominated by service clubs, ratepayers' associations, women's groups, trade unions, private interest organizations and, in the 1930s, by the Social Credit Party. The city councils of the 1920-40 period were a combination of interest groups associated loosely with the CGA or Labour or purporting to be independent of both. In this respect, and considering the sensitive financial situation, the position of mayor called for special abilities.

Calgary had three mayors between 1922 and 1945. All were positive characters with well-developed political consciences. Two of them, George Webster (1922-26) and Andrew Davison (1930-45), epitomized the type of popular leadership needed to sustain public confidence in times of financial stringency. Both were extremely popular and were elected to the Provincial Legislature during their mayoralty. Webster was elected president of the Board of Trade in 1923 and consistently topped the polls as alderman. Although he was a successful businessman and a Liberal, Webster was deeply concerned with extricating the city from its financial difficulties. He believed that poor land policies were at the heart of Calgary's problems and stressed the need for sensible, long-term legislation to control land speculation. Under Webster, the city's restricted growth policies received fullest rein. His move from municipal to provincial politics in 1926 was considered a major loss to Calgary.

Davison, an Irishman who came to Edmonton in 1895, was fond of referring to himself as an "Edmonton boy who became mayor of Calgary". He was elected mayor by acclamation in 1929, after an aldermanic career spanning eight years, and on four other occasions was unchallenged for the mayoralty. Previously employed by the *Herald* as a linotype operator, he was the first mayor of Calgary who was neither a businessman nor a member of the professions. In 1933, Davison led a Labour-inspired move by refusing to pay the United States exchange on city bonds. The eventual saving to the city was an estimated $350,000. He was also the driving force behind Calgary's adoption of the Fortin Refinancing Plan in 1937. When elected to the Provincial Legislature during his term of office, Davison held both positions concurrently.

Calgary's third mayor during this period was Fred Osborne, who served from 1927 to 1929. As a former bookseller, Osborne occupied a middle ground between Webster's successful business appeal and Davison's identification with labour.

The presence of opposing interest groups on city council eliminated some of the elitism previously associated with local government in Calgary. Policies were now implemented which more closely represented popular consensus. Labour's major success in 1922 came after a CGA-dominated council had suggested wage reductions for civic employees. Labour aldermen resisted the curtailment of streetcar service, particularly on the unprofitable Ogden Line, and guarded workers' interests by demanding union rates from all companies doing business with the city. In 1923, council explored the allegation that Imperial Oil was not paying plumbers union rates on the construction site of its Calgary refinery. The Labour bloc also tried to secure consideration for civic employees working unusual hours. On the other hand, the influence of the CGA could be seen in pared-down expenditures. The high relief costs of the 1930s were subject to careful scrutiny by CGA aldermen who were generally more conscious of abuses than their Labour colleagues.

The growing complexity of municipal government became apparent at this point in Calgary's history. The Board of Public Utilities became increasingly involved in municipal affairs, as agreements with companies supplying electricity and gas grew more complicated and acrimonious. The gas company, in particular, continued its bitter disputes with the city over rates and franchise rights. It was a time when Calgary, struggling under a tremendous financial burden, looked to the provincial government for relief in the form of loans or, preferably, a more equitable distribution of taxing power.

The period between the wars witnessed the birth and development of movements designed to bring attention to inequities in Canadian society. In western Canada, these protests carried

Members of the 1915 Calgary police force in front of the four-storey brick police station on Seventh Avenue S.E.

The Calgary ski jump, erected at the east end of the grandstand on the Exhibition grounds in 1920. Its success was short-lived, due to the unpredictability of Calgary's winters.

British sports traditions were strong in Calgary, and snow was no deterrent to a serious rugby match.

additional overtones of regional disparity, the most obvious manifestation of which was the progressivist movement. However, the voice of agrarian discontent was not confined to the federal Progressives. The United Farmers of Alberta and the movement towards co-operation represented further attempts to unify the farm effort. The ideals of socialism, too, gained in popularity, culminating in the formation of the Co-operative Commonwealth Federation in 1932. Calgary provided the urban base from which many of these reform movements were organized and gained momentum. If Edmonton functioned as Alberta's centre of government, Calgary clearly emerged as the voice of political alternatives.

In 1921, the United Farmers of Alberta toppled the Liberals from office in Edmonton. Despite its rural orientation, the UFA was based in Calgary and enjoyed the support of Labour leaders in the city. A. Ross, Calgary Labour MLA, became minister for public works in the UFA's first cabinet. Henry Wise Wood, the inspirational leader of the UFA, was identified more with Calgary than with his home town, Carstairs. Wood was a fascinating figure. Largely self-educated, he had read widely in theories of social change and translated his personal philosophy into the ideals of the UFA. Wood believed that government by a coalition of representative occupational groups was a necessary prerequisite to the defeat of competition. His theory of co-operation was the governing spirit behind the Alberta brand of federal Progressive thought. Under Wood's guidance, the UFA formed many co-operative ventures, most of which, like the Alberta Wheat Pool, were located in Calgary.

Although the UFA's failure to implement Wood's theory of group government was apparent by 1924, the United Farmers continued to govern the province as a rural party. Calgary representatives in Edmonton between 1921 and 1935 included three representatives of Labour, five Conservatives, three Liberals and two Independents. None achieved any particular distinction. Even the success of William Irvine as Calgary's first successful Labour representative in Ottawa reflected a rural spillover into urban voting patterns.

Irvine was a volatile, highly contentious figure, whose writings and speeches made him a spokesman for radical change. While his social theories were complementary to those of Wood, Irvine concentrated on the rights of labour. The author of numerous articles and other publications and elected as MP for east Calgary in 1921, Irvine symbolized a unifying force in Calgary labour circles. He was a perennial speaker at radical gatherings, and his advice and support were sought by Labour aldermanic candidates. Later, Irvine contributed to the formation of the CCF and became a strong supporter of J. S. Woodsworth.

Irvine's electoral success in 1921 was rooted in his rural affiliations. In 1920, he had published his controversial book, *Farmers in Politics.* As editor of the *Nutcracker* as well as subsequent journals in Calgary, he continued to support the ideals of the Labour Party and the Non-Partisan League. When the Non-Partisan League was absorbed into the UFA, Irvine became the party's chief publicist. In the election of 1921, he enjoyed the full support of the UFA, which at a special meeting decided to support Irvine in Calgary East, where he had run as a Labour candidate in 1917 and been easily defeated.[36] In return, Labour promised its support for the UFA-endorsed candidate in Calgary West. Aided by a strong rural vote, Irvine was elected, only to be beaten four years later by a Conservative. His defeat was attributed partly to the fact that the boundaries in his east Calgary riding had been re-drawn, resulting in the loss of many rural voters.[37] Irvine was again successful in 1926 at Wetaskiwin, running as a farmers' candidate, and it was in this capacity that he became identified in federal politics with the radical Ginger Group.

In a way, Irvine was a product of the turbulence in Calgary society. Disenchanted organizations, like the One Big Union or the Co-operative Commonwealth Federation, also found expression in Calgary's urban environment. But radical ideals of worker equality were not consistently popular. Calgary preferred political alternatives that reflected the aspirations of rural Alberta. In this respect, the rise of Social Credit represented an evolutionary trend in Calgary's urban development.

Just as the philosophical Wood epitomized the UFA, so did the charismatic William Aberhart personify the Social Credit movement.[38] Aberhart's party entered provincial politics in 1935, ousting the tired, disillusioned farmers' government. Using oratorical skills honed in the classroom and the pulpit, the magnetic Aberhart preached political salvation through monetary miracles. Aberhart was a Calgary school principal and a superb

The Empress Theatre was a thriving vaudeville attraction in the 1920s.

Calgary boasted at least six movie houses in the 1930s.

Bowness Park swimming pool, August 1930. During the Depression, Bowness Park became a holiday spot for many Calgary residents. On weekends during the height of summer, two streetcars left the centre of town every 15 minutes taking people to the park. The ride cost ten cents and admission to the park was five cents.

organizer, with a flair for the dramatic. His radio preaching was the first effective use in western Canada of a mass medium that was still relatively new. His voice carried over the air waves to thousands of listeners throughout the province, most of whom were organized into Bible study groups. Through the Prophetic Bible Institute in Calgary, Aberhart's precepts were passed on to dedicated younger followers. So, when Aberhart decided to take up the cause of Social Credit in 1932, he headed a potential political organization of considerable magnitude.

Unlike the UFA, Social Credit appealed to a wide cross section of the electorate. Both town and country voted for Aberhart in 1935 and continued to elect Social Credit governments for over a generation. Although the Social Credit movement was born in the city, it had an evangelical, fundamentalist appeal that found best expression in the less sophisticated rural areas. Over the years, Social Credit became increasingly identified with rural Alberta and did not, in fact, focus on specific urban needs and problems. Social Credit developed in response to a general need, and Calgary, by providing the impetus, continued in its traditional role as spokesman for a provincial consensus that was still fundamentally rural.

Unlike the United Farmers, Social Credit was able to effectively siphon off the potential labour vote. When the UFA was in power, it formed an alliance with, but did not absorb, organized labour. Social Credit was much more successful in this regard, but was never very popular with Calgary businessmen, who feared for the future of investment capital in the city. Most viewed the Aberhart phenomenon first with disdain, later with perplexity and always with fond hopes of an early return to sanity.[39] On the other hand, Social Credit was traditionally strong in working class districts of the city where the party's promises to topple elitist institutions were well received. The failure of the labour movement in Calgary in 1920-35 can be explained in part by the Social Credit phenomenon and its utopian ideals.

Calgary's urban character was now established. An interesting aspect of this development was the degree to which the city reflected a self-imposed frontier image as opposed to the sophistication and anonymity associated with growing urban status. Calgary society retained a strong identification with the outdoors

and remained in tune with conservative rural Alberta. The society also exhibited an aggressive buoyancy which never seemed to waver in its aspirations for big city status.

Slow population growth restricted Calgary's size and enabled the city to retain much of its frontier flavour. Chance meetings by acquaintances in the downtown area were common, and while service and recreational amenities expanded, they were few enough in number to foster close social interaction. The resident business community was close-knit and not yet fractured by the occupational dissimilarities that marked later years. The Board of Trade remained a viable forum of local business sentiment. The small city image was reinforced by personal gossip items in the press, identification with local sporting teams and the unifying element of the Stampede, which during these years was more completely a Calgary production.

Calgary's small size and relative ethnic homogeneity contributed to the development of a conservative social order. Economic disparities were on too small a scale to produce a sustained ground swell of radical sentiment. Furthermore, the financial barrenness of the period resulted in institutional development along conservative lines. Here, growth was under the direction of long-tenured individuals who represented both authority and stability. Police Chief David Ritchie (1919-1941) and Superintendent of Schools Melville Scott (1906-35) presided over their respective organizations with a moral force that was rarely questioned. The general lack of mobility meant fewer job changes, with the result that minor positions of authority with the city, the school board and the police force were filled by individuals who matured in the same position. The institutional voice of authority commanded more respect in Calgary than in centres where the population was larger, more mobile and certainly more diverse in occupation or origin.

The relative lack of cultural facilities also reinforced Calgary's identification with the frontier and the outdoors. To a degree, this situation was aggravated by the absence of a university, which normally would have fostered cultural institutions. The art department of the Provincial Institute of Technology attempted to provide cultural leadership. Through the able guidance of people like A.C. (Ace) Leighton, Lars Hawkaness and others, this body raised artistic standards and encouraged local talent.

However, those youngsters who showed promise in the arts were sent away to study, and it was not until 1946 that the Calgary Allied Arts Council opened facilities in the former Mount Royal residence of Eugene Coste.

If public encouragement for the arts seemed spasmodic and slow, Calgarians seemed to take a genuine pride in their city's outdoor attractions. By the late 1920s, Calgary's potential as a tourist centre was realized, and efforts were made to promote the city as a jumping-off point to nearby scenic attractions and hunting grounds. Calgary's affiliation with the livestock industry was not allowed to die. The fact that many individuals resident in Calgary had been true frontiersmen added a touch of authenticity. Journals like *Canadian Cattlemen* published nostalgic reminiscences and nourished the spirit of the frontier.

An aggressive quality was alive in Calgary in these years and partly explained the city's unique urban character. As the urban manifestation of both livestock and oil enterprises, Calgary reflected a continued faith in opportunism. The quickness with which civic officials responded to an economic upsurge showed how ready they were to risk large sums for desirable amenities. The Glenmore Reservoir project in 1929 was an excellent example of this tendency. Exploratory activities in Turner Valley tantalized Calgary's dreams of general prosperity and great personal wealth. However, Turner Valley was uncertain enough to encourage only the more persistent gamblers.

By the outbreak of World War II, Calgary was a western Canadian city with a distinctive character. Most of this individuality could be explained by the city's association with two individualistic and high-risk industries. It was also partly a function of size, age and frontier influences. Calgary was a regional city, and while aspects of social unrest made it resemble Toronto more than High River, it remained primarily an urban expression of southern Alberta.

Chapter Four

City in Transition
1948-1965

After 1947, Calgary experienced a sustained period of phenomenal urban growth. Explained partly in terms of national prosperity, Calgary's expansion was also linked to the discovery of substantial petroleum deposits in Alberta, beginning with Leduc-Woodbend in 1947 and continuing through the 1950s with Redwater, Pembina, Swan Hills and other fields. The impact of the oil boom threw Calgary into a period of major redirection in urban development. The transition was observable by the mid 1960s, when Calgary emerged as the Canadian headquarters of an international industry which had begun to probe areas beyond Alberta. The new Calgary bore little resemblance physically to the city of the 1940s. Towering skyscrapers, sprawling subdivisions and regional shopping centres indicated both growth and affluence. Yet the most significant change between 1945 and 1965 was not in the city's appearance or in the nature of its labour force. The crucial difference was that the new Calgary no longer reflected the productivity and mentality of its hinterland. It now stood separate, and in this sense had achieved a new urban status.

ECONOMIC GROWTH AND METROPOLITAN DEVELOPMENT

In this period, Alberta shifted its economic dependence from agriculture to mining. In 1945, agriculture accounted for over half of Alberta's wealth, while in the same year mining products contributed approximately 10 per cent. By 1965, agriculture's share had dropped to 23 per cent, and mining accounted for 31 per cent of Alberta's net value of production. In 1947, sales from Alberta oil and gas and related production totalled $20.3 million.

By 1965, the corresponding figure exceeded $704 million, and three years later topped the one billion dollar mark (Appendix, Table X).[1]

Calgary soon consolidated its position as national headquarters for this highly profitable industry.[2] Out of the complex network of petroleum exploration, extraction, financing, processing and marketing, Calgary emerged as a head office centre. By 1965, there were 965 industry headquarters in Calgary, ranging from large multi-national corporations to small two- and three-man companies. As a head office centre, Calgary was able to eclipse its traditional rival, Edmonton, which became increasingly identified with oilfield supply and service, and by the mid 1960s Calgary's association with the oil and gas industry had given it the third highest number of head offices in the country.

Calgary's earlier connections with oil development in Turner Valley gave it the head start it needed to offset Edmonton's greater proximity to the producing fields and its advantage as Alberta's political administrative centre. Well-known in the oil and gas industry by 1947, Calgary quickly adapted to the increased activity after that date. Temporary office space was created, and rapid construction provided necessary services. The Calgary Petroleum Club, formed in 1948 by American and Canadian oilmen and first located in the Palliser Hotel, focussed on the social side of the oil business. By the mid 1950s, when exploratory activity was at its height, Calgary capitalized on these initial advantages. The need for co-ordinated efforts, the opportunity to engage in joint ventures and the presence of amenities and services led to an increasing concentration of oil activity in Calgary.

Local oilmen operating from Calgary were active in exploration during these years. Probably the most successful was Robert A.

Brown Jr., the son of the persistent pioneer who had discovered oil in Turner Valley in 1936. Through a series of mergers, Brown created Home Oil Company Ltd. in 1955, and within a decade it was Canada's only independently owned major oil company. Home Oil made five substantial oil and gas discoveries in Alberta, including the rich Beaverhill Lake formation. By the mid 1960s, Brown had moved his company's interests beyond Alberta to the North Sea, mining operations in British Columbia and marketing of natural gas in the United States.

Other industries related to the oil and gas industry were developed in Calgary during this period. Bruce Nodwell's Calgary company pioneered the tracked vehicle in Canada during the 1950s while working with Imperial Oil near Cynthia, Alberta. In the mid 1960s the amalgamated firm of Robinson-Nodwell Manufacturing Company was designing and building the world's largest tracked vehicles.[3] The vast distances and isolation associated with exploratory activities gave birth to Atco Industries, a world leader in mobile living unit construction.[4] From a capital base of $4,000, Calgary's Ron Southern built Atco into an innovative enterprise and an outstanding example of manufacturing adaptation to a special market.

At this point, the Canadian oil and gas industry was Alberta-oriented with at least one major field yet to be discovered. The industry had not achieved the global dimensions which would later thrust Calgary into a more international role. Important decisions on regional development emanated from Calgary, and resident oilmen were the most interested in northern development. By 1965, as data processing firms, investment consultants and pipeline manufacturers continued to base their operations in the city, Calgary had become an "oil city".

An oil boom population flooded Calgary, and virtually no aspect of internal economic growth remained unaffected by developments in the industry. Expansions in educational services, construction, retailing and manufacturing all reflected the dynamic growth of oil and gas enterprises. An estimated seven jobs were generated for every individual employed in the oil business.[5] By 1965, about half of Calgary's work force owed their jobs to oil and gas, and Calgary had become inextricably dependent on a single industry.

In other areas, Calgary's economic development continued

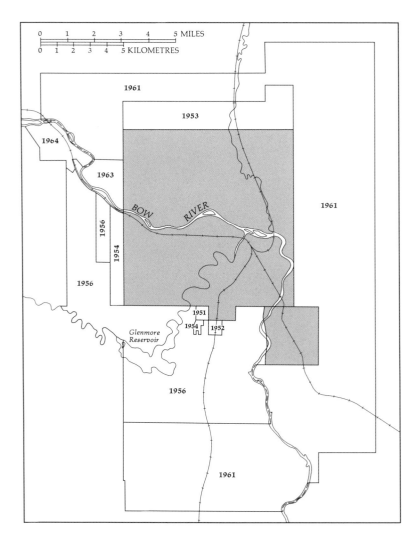

8 Boundary Extensions, 1912-1965

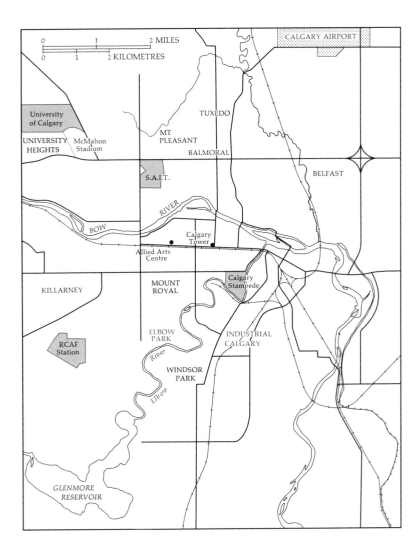

9 Calgary in 1965

along traditional lines. Agricultural produce remained an important component of the city's economic base and accounted for approximately 20 per cent of all manufacturing establishments and a much higher proportion of the total value of production. The food and beverage industry, by catering to regional and extra-regional demands, revealed the growing importance of Calgary's position in the national economy. In another sense, this industry underscored Calgary's reliance on the primary sector. Most other manufacturing enterprises in the city represented the final stages of an assemblage process originating elsewhere. Calgary's position as a regional distributor, dependent upon production processes in other parts of North America, remained unchanged.[6]

The relatively minor role played by manufacturing in Calgary had its corollary in the tremendous growth of the service industry. Even discounting construction, service industries accounted for well over half of the work force in the mid 1960s. But Calgary's economy was obviously not self-sustaining, for much of the service sector grew in response to income generated by the oil and gas industries.

The presence of a flourishing construction industry continued to be a major factor in Calgary's economic life. Housing and office-complex construction created resident millionaires, furnished employment for approximately 10 per cent of the labour force and gave rise to locally based housing corporations. By 1965, the effects of the construction industry were reflected in the changing face of the downtown area and in the modern subdivisions which swelled the city boundaries (see Maps 8, 9).

In other spheres of economic activity, Calgary's influence did not increase greatly. The westward grain route to the Pacific grew in importance after 1945, but Calgary's role was virtually unchanged by the increased volume of statutory grain traffic to the terminal elevators in Vancouver. Cattle remained a risky enterprise, and that industry failed to assert itself as a stable influence on Calgary's economy. Wide fluctuations in supply and demand and the growing complexity of management problems almost led Burns Foods Ltd. into bankruptcy in the mid 1960s. The introduction of exotic breeds, together with the growing emphasis on grain-feeding operations, meant smaller, more intensive operations. This, in turn, led to the entrance into the

A new era in Calgary's development began in February 1947 when Leduc No. 1 "blew in". This strike ushered in a major oil boom that could not have come at a more opportune time. Production from the Turner Valley field had begun to decline, and Calgary refineries were on the verge of arranging crude oil imports from the United States. But with the Leduc discovery, Alberta once again had an oil surplus, and Calgary could continue as the administrative and financial centre of the Canadian petroleum industry.

Although Calgary's dependence on its rural hinterland was lessened considerably by the oil and gas industry, the city did maintain its traditional role as a regional distributing centre in the years after World War II. The Calgary Farm Machinery and Supply Company was one city firm that depended on the surrounding area for business.

(845-28)
R 1370

Projects such as the Trans-Canada
Pipeline helped stimulate Calgary's
rapid growth in the post-war period. In
1965, the head offices of 965 oil and
oil-related companies and branch offices
of an additional 336 were located in the
city. The benefits of being the nation's
petroleum capital continue to enhance
Calgary in the 1970s.

cattle industry of individuals whose principal revenue came from other sources.

By 1965, Calgary had clearly emerged as an oil and gas centre of considerable magnitude, but its economic base remained very narrow. However, the need for a diversified economy seemed more theoretical than actual, for the economic largesse from the oil and gas industry was still very visible. Here, the long-range policy of Burns Foods Ltd. to decrease its dependence on meat-packing operations anticipated future trends. No longer dependent upon the agricultural prosperity of a rural hinterland to fuel its internal economy, Calgary now depended on an industry which itself was still essentially geared towards exploration and extraction.

POPULATION GROWTH AND ETHNIC RELATIONSHIPS

Statistics speak clearly on the phenomenal growth of the city's population between 1946-65. In these two decades, Calgary rose from a small provincial city to an urban metropolis similar to Ottawa-Hull, Hamilton or even its prairie rival, Winnipeg. In 1946, fewer than 100,000 lived in Calgary. By 1965, the figure stood at 315,680 and represented an annual increase of over 5.8 per cent (Appendix, Tables III, IV). Three features of this population expansion warrant special attention. The first concerns the solidification of an American influence long observable in the city. The second lies in the peculiar nature of the work force, which was more white-collar oriented and affluent than in typical Canadian metropolitan centres. The third feature is essentially demographic and involves the superimposition of a sizeable immigrant population onto a relatively small nucleus of Calgary-born residents.

Calgary is probably the most "Americanized" of all Canadian cities. Strong north-south links have been traditional since the days of the open range. Calgary's association with the oil and gas industry accentuated this strong liaison with the United States. Under the influence of American oilmen, Calgary emerged as one of the most continental of North American cities. By 1965, over 30,000 Americans lived in the city, with their numbers directed towards the higher income brackets. They figured prominently in the city's social and economic life, and in many ways Calgary has

more in common with Tulsa or Houston than with Toronto, Montreal or Hamilton. Although much of the "Americanization" of Calgary has been part of a national phenomenon, the actual movement of personnel and capital across the border to Calgary's "oil patch" has created tangible cultural and economic bonds with the United States.

The rapid growth of Calgary's labour force after 1951 produced an inflationary spiral which, by 1954, made Calgary the most expensive of 10 regional centres. In 1961, the work force had increased 82.68 per cent over the previous decade, with considerable emphasis on the growing female working population. The resulting rise in family incomes was accompanied by more stable growth conditions in the 1960s. By 1965, Calgarians enjoyed the highest annual income of any centre in Alberta and one of the highest in the country. Calgary dropped from tenth to sixth on the consumer price index, making its residents among the nation's most affluent citizens. Wages paid to the city's 109,000 workers topped $343 million in 1965.[7]

Occupational structure changed little. The continuing reliance on trade and commerce resulted in a preponderance of the professional and managerial classes. The substantial numbers of unskilled labourers who work on the assembly lines of major industrial centres are conspicuously absent in Calgary. The ratio of managerial to unskilled labour in the city, at about three to one, is the highest of any large city in the country. The unchanging nature of the work force since 1911 has been an enduring feature in Calgary's development and is rooted in the city's role as the commercial centre of Alberta. The high income of tradesmen, particularly those in the construction industry, combined with an increasing number of working women has modified socioeconomic disparities. Calgary's 1965 work force probably possessed a degree of economic homogeneity on a level unmatched anywhere in Canada.

A significant factor in Calgary's population increase after 1950 was the degree and source of its migrant influx. Between the years 1948-59, immigration was responsible for almost 70 per cent of the total population increase, while in 1951-61 an annual average of over 8,000 new citizens entered Calgary. The many annexations to the city's area between 1951 and 1965 did not add appreciably to the total population. When Forest Lawn,

Montgomery and Bowness were added to the city between 1961 and 1964, their total population was fewer than 20,000. The importance of immigration to Calgary's growth is emphasized by the fact that the city's birthrate declined steadily after 1954, when it had peaked at 31.8 births per 1,000.

Most of the immigration to Calgary since 1945 came from other Canadian provinces, with neighbouring Saskatchewan and Manitoba being the major sources. Only with British Columbia and Ontario has the rate of population exchange remained the same (Appendix, Table V). Although Calgary continued to receive immigrants from Great Britain and the United States, the numbers from Europe were negligible by the 1960s (Appendix, Tables VI, VII). It is difficult to measure the degree of urban drift from surrounding rural areas, although it does appear as if Calgary received many new residents from smaller Alberta centres. Between the years 1961-66, the six census divisions that comprise southern Alberta all experienced absolute decreases in population. Only the census division occupied by Calgary recorded a population increase. In the decade 1951-61, five of these census divisions counted a total of over 20,000 immigrants. The establishment of regional planning bodies in the 1950s to provide for more orderly growth patterns was partly a response to problems caused by urban drift.[8]

Most of Calgary's population is Canadian-born. The figure hovers around 80 per cent with at least half the absolute total being born in Alberta. In terms of ethnic origin, Calgary has retained its position as having one of the highest percentages of Anglo-Saxons of any major city in the country. Of the other ethnic groups, Germans are most numerous, followed by small numbers of Scandinavians, French, Dutch, Ukrainians, Polish and Italians. However, a significant proportion of these people are fluent only in English, indicating that many of them were born in Canada.

Some residential patterns associated with ethnic origins were observable in Calgary. People of Anglo-Saxon origin predominated in the more affluent southwest and northwest sections of the city. On the other hand, Forest Lawn, the lower-priced residential area annexed in the 1960s, was far more cosmopolitan. Indeed, the northeast quadrant of the city, with the largest proportions of German, Italian and Ukrainian residents, was the only area to boast a degree of ethnic heterogeneity. In the downtown district, a viable Chinatown had existed unchanged since 1910.

THE URBAN LANDSCAPE

Demands associated with rapid growth produced significant changes in the physical face of the city. Boundaries expanded to take in suburban areas, and a high-density commercial district literally rose out of the old business core. Formal planning was introduced into the machinery of civic administration, and changing transportation and residential priorities redirected traditional growth patterns (see Map 11).

Beginning with the annexation of Windsor Park in 1951, Calgary expanded rapidly. In a series of six annexations before 1965, Calgary's corporate area swelled from approximately 40 to 155.8 square miles. Municipal planning played an important part in directing this development, though by 1960, when the city's supply of building land was all but exhausted, the role of the private developer had become increasingly important. The 1950s witnessed a growing awareness on the part of provincial and municipal legislators of the need to plan for orderly growth. Legislation at both levels resulted in the establishment of a city planning department with far greater powers than its previous counterparts, which had functioned primarily in an advisory capacity. While the planning department's primary mandate was to specify the nature and scope of Calgary's internal growth, there was also a need to co-ordinate this development within a regional context.

A definite trend during this period was the steady deterioration of certain inner city areas. Heterogeneous land-use patterns were allowed to develop, with the result that by 1965 some downtown areas faced uncertain futures. In 1964, it was estimated that approximately 40 per cent of the city's labour force worked in the downtown area, but the resident population was a meagre two to three per cent of the city total. Aware of the problems faced in preserving the identity and function of the inner city, civic officials, in 1966, introduced the Downtown Master Plan as a blueprint for future development. An essential part of this plan was the need to restore the residential component of the city core.

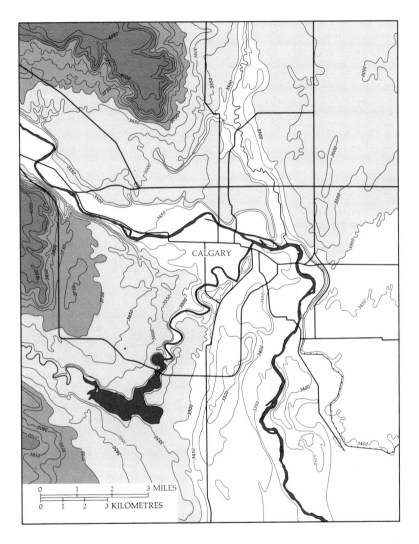

10 Topographical Features

City planners concentrated on developing a high-density business area. Lateral commercial expansion was easily contained in a relatively small area west of the established retail district. The slow process of land-use deterioration in adjacent areas, already observable before 1940, continued unchecked. The civic policy of incidental re-zoning was also a contributing factor. So by 1965, the closely defined main business district was more isolated than ever, separated from the rest of the city by the railroad, the river and an area of dwindling taxation revenues. The city's unsuccessful 1965 negotiations with the CPR to re-route the mainline along the Bow River represented one of the few serious attempts to re-shape the pattern of commercial development in downtown Calgary.

Although the downtown area remained the centre of commercial activity, the implementation of new planning policies greatly reduced its importance as a service and retail centre. The neighbourhood-unit concept of residential living called for functional land use which would create communities by building in necessary services. By the mid 1960s the neighbourhood-unit principle was expanded into the sector concept of planned growth. This was a general plan for overall development within a specified large area, and it established guidelines within which private developers could operate. Provisions were included to ensure adequate recreational areas and schools and to encourage the emergence of shopping plazas which could rival the downtown area in variety and quality of services.[9]

Calgarians displayed a marked preference for single family dwellings, and this factor, combined with the steadily increasing population, induced developers to acquire land farther and farther away from the city centre. They were aided in their efforts by a number of factors, including the co-operation of civic officials in providing necessary services to new communities. Certainly the city's large annexations in the early 1960s contributed to the "unlimited space" concept which was to prevail throughout the decade. As the energy behind land development switched to the private domain in the 1960s, a change occurred in the way residential districts were differentiated. Access to public transportation and the presence of utilities were no longer distinguishing factors, for the automobile had replaced the streetcar as the most popular form of transportation and the extension of utilities had become a prerequisite for all new housing construction. Exclusive new districts emerged in conjunction with the establishment of the University of Calgary in the early 1960s. With little naturally scenic land on the city's periphery, private developers began to create environmental attractions to enhance the exclusiveness of their subdivisions.[10] The enforcement of consistent building regulations, combined with the preference of Calgarians for single dwelling units, resulted in the steady growth of well-planned, attractive communities. Between 1948 and 1965, over 60,000 homes were constructed, making Calgary one of the nation's leaders in single family housing.[11]

There was also a substantial increase in the construction of apartments. These were concentrated mainly in the inner city area, particularly between the CPR mainline and Seventeenth Avenue South where they contributed to high-density residence and to multiple land use. By 1965, some of the pre-World War II apartment blocks had assumed the squalid appearance usually associated with tenement buildings in older cities.

Another aspect of rapid urban growth during this period was friction between Calgary and its surrounding rural areas. Neighbouring towns and villages were being drawn into Calgary's growth syndrome, and it was felt that the provincial government should take steps to secure the future of these small communities in the face of Calgary's expansion. On the other hand, Calgary civic authorities were determined that the city should not be swamped by commuters who lived on the city edges but did not pay city taxes. In 1953, the provincial government established a Regional Planning Commission to ensure sound regional planning under a single administrative and political structure. In these years, however, the commission possessed neither the desire nor the authority to make it an effective agency.[12] Originally, the commission's financial support and membership were on a voluntary basis, with the result that it functioned as a composite body of representatives from cities, towns, villages, rural municipalities and improvement districts. But beyond approving authority for subdivisions and advising on zoning and development, the commission received little encouragement from its members. The fact that real power was wielded only by the provincial government certainly contributed to the half-hearted efforts of the Regional Planning Commission.

Calgary's physical growth had not slowed by 1965, and economic indices pointed to continued expansion. Some aspects of Calgary's physical transition were observable, however. While the integration of rural-urban development had not occurred, it was apparent that new growth strategies for Calgary itself were evolving. New transportation corridors like the Blackfoot and Sarcee Trails formed the nucleus of a ring-road complex which diverted traffic concentration from the high-density areas. The inflexibility of the zoning principle was seen as prohibitive to effective planning. Instead, development control was gaining credibility, as evidenced by the sector concept of new area planning. On the other hand, adverse effects of zoning were seen in the inner city area where deteriorating land use was increasingly apparent. The expansion of Calgary in the early 1960s to include the surrounding communities of Forest Lawn and Bowness relieved some of the land pressure and signalled the end of direct civic control over physical expansion through corporate land ownership. The day of the private developer had arrived with all its implications for civic policy-making.

THE URBAN COMMUNITY: SOCIAL AND POLITICAL LIFE

Rapid growth had effected little change in Calgary's political climate by 1965. On the provincial level, while the urbanization of Alberta was enhanced by the growth of Calgary and Edmonton, the hold of the rural-oriented Social Credit Party remained unchanged since the Depression. In municipal politics, the general affluence and rising population made it possible to implement expensive growth programs. A definite absence of heated public issues was partially offset by the continuing success of colourful individuals at the polls.

Calgarians of the 1950-65 era seemed more apathetic than ever towards politics and civic issues in particular. Labour became a token force in city council in the 1950s. Elected commissioners disappeared in 1952 with little public reaction, even though ratepayers in the past had consistently voted against the concept of government by appointment. There was no public pressure and little rationale behind council's decision to return to the ward system in 1960. Election statistics for all levels of government indicated that for an increasing number of Calgarians the option of the franchise was irrelevant. Voting patterns at both the

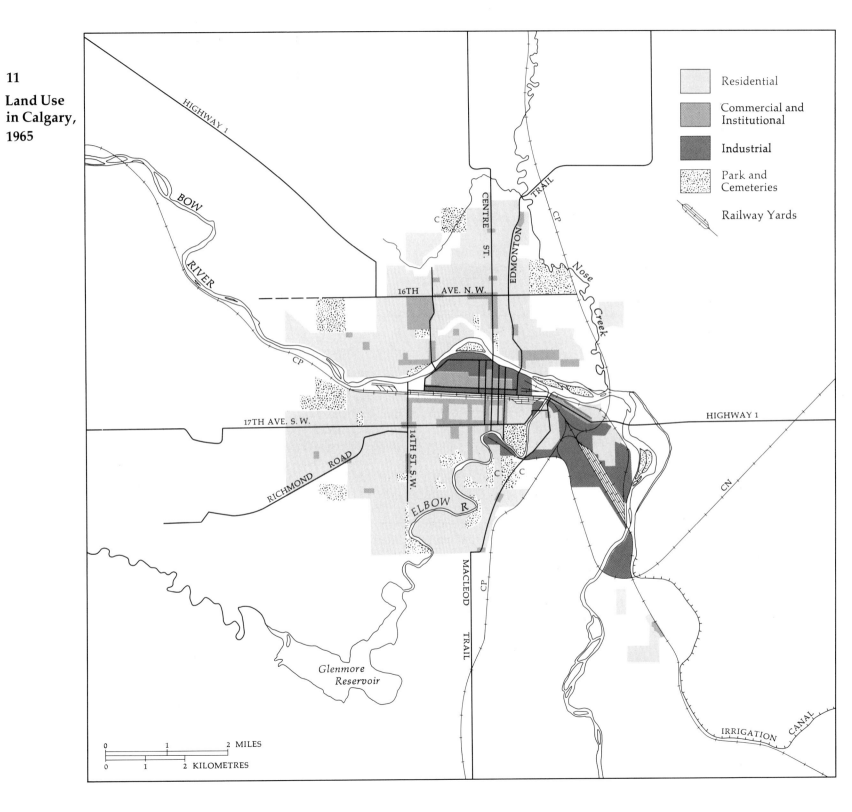

11

**Land Use
in Calgary,
1965**

Residential

Commercial and
Institutional

Industrial

Park and
Cemeteries

Railway Yards

HIGHWAY 1

BOW

RIVER

CP

CENTRE ST.

EDMONTON TRAIL

CP

Nose Creek

C

16TH   AVE. N.W.

17TH AVE. S.W.

HIGHWAY 1

RICHMOND ROAD

14TH ST. S.W.

ELBOW R

C   C

MACLEOD TRAIL

CP

CN

Glenmore
Reservoir

IRRIGATION   CANAL

0   1   2 MILES

0   1   2 KILOMETRES

provincial and civic levels appeared habitual and reflected the enduring appeal of individuals identified with social conservatism. Calgary's general voting patterns remained complementary to those of rural Alberta, and no typically urban differential had emerged by 1965.

The relatively homogeneous nature of Calgary's population meant a continuation of the Conservative tradition in federal politics. Over the years, Calgary exhibited a voting pattern that was southern Albertan in scope. It was rooted in a belief that the Conservative Party was a greater friend than the Liberals, who were seen as both pro-Quebec and out of sympathy with western sentiment. The expansion of the oil and gas industry into the North added another dimension to Calgary's traditional Conservatism. As the industry shifted its attention to potential reserves beyond Alberta, Calgary became increasingly affected by federal government decisions on leases and regulations. At the same time, the discovery of the major producing fields put greater emphasis on expensive exploratory programs financed by American capital. So while Calgary's economic lifeline ran increasingly north-south, it also became more vulnerable to political decisions coming from Ottawa. But since resident oilmen were sceptical of the willingness of either political party to provide for the long-range goals of the oil and gas industry, Calgary's continuing allegiance to the Conservative Party can be seen as apolitical and uncommitted, as well as traditional.

It has been said that the provincial Social Credit Party floated to success on a sea of oil, and certainly the windfall it received through royalty payments helped sustain the party's popular appeal. Its sympathetic attitude towards private enterprise also bolstered its image as a friend of the oil and gas industry. So it was not surprising that under the able leadership of Ernest Manning the Social Credit Party continued to dominate provincial legislatures throughout the post-war period. Indeed, for as long as Manning exploited his considerable charismatic powers to combine religion and politics, the Social Credit Party appeared unbeatable. By 1965, despite the growing urban orientation of Alberta, no political substitute had emerged.[13] It is probably valid to assert that the appeal of individualism, combined with a solid administrative record, helped sustain the popularity of Social Credit in Calgary between 1944 and 1968.

However, any attempt to correlate socio-economic variables with voting patterns in the city falls short of the mark. A dominant theme in Social Credit campaigns was its strong anti-socialist stand. Yet Calgary's wealthiest districts were least inclined to elect Social Credit candidates, preferring instead to cast their votes for Liberals. On the other hand, the CCF and, later, the NDP made few inroads into predominantly Social Credit majorities in working class districts.

General prosperity in the 1950s enabled municipal governments to provide all the amenities associated with large cities. Schools, parks, swimming pools and other community services expanded rapidly to meet growing needs. The increased borrowing powers which accompanied higher assessments kept both the mill rate and public resentment down. It was also a period of colourful municipal leadership. Mayor Don Mackay (1950-59) was a classic personification of turn-of-the-century boosterism born anew. Immensely popular, he typified the promotional effervescence that had distinguished early Calgary mayors like Wesley Orr or, more appropriately, James Reilly. Harry Hays, mayor from 1959 to 1963, also had his precedents. Like Daniel Webster Marsh in 1889, Hays was a popular and successful cattleman and was expected to provide the common-sense leadership of the practical businessman. John Walter Grant MacEwan (1963-65) probably best symbolized Calgary's affiliation with the true western character. The versatile MacEwan, with his scrupulous ethical code and frugal approach to government, offered a personal example of the fundamental values he preached.

The appeal of individuals like Mackay, Hays and MacEwan has reinforced Calgary's frontier image in modern times. It was Mackay who advertised the white stetson as Calgary's emblem. Harry Hays personally served his liquid concoction of dubious origin to thousands at his annual breakfast during the Calgary Stampede. And it was MacEwan who nurtured a western identification through his many books on frontierlife, including a history of Calgary. The distinctively western flavour of Calgary was consciously cultivated during the post-war period, and although by 1965 its population approached big city status, Calgary, for many people, retained its historic frontier image. The city's annual flood of tourists focussed on the Stampede and the nostalgia of the early West, and Calgary was so successful in perpetuat-

Bartenders on strike, marching east along Eighth Avenue between First and Second Streets S.W., 1948.

Crescent Heights Public Library in the late 1940s. Calgary's rapid growth in the decades after 1945 has meant that the city has had difficulty providing services to its burgeoning population.

ing a distinctive personality that it has invited emulation. Certainly, Edmonton's Klondike Days represents a conscious attempt to rival Calgary's success.

In many ways, the oil and gas industry superimposed an aggressive self-confidence onto this frontier character. Optimism has always been part of Calgary's heritage, but since 1950 the city has assumed a vibrancy associated with economic success. It is probably for this reason that of all Canadian cities Calgary is most easily equated with the popular notion of American materialism. But the frontier image also exhibited negative features. The Calgary of 1965 lacked the cosmopolitanism of most large urban centres. While there were plenty of good steak houses, there were few restaurants serving continental foods. The fledgling university, opened in 1960, made little impact on the city's cultural life, and many newcomers lamented the absence of opportunities to pursue the arts. It was said that people did not seem to care. A plebiscite on a new public library had been twice defeated in the 1950s, even though the existing Carnegie facility was clearly inadequate. Calgary possessed only one concert hall of note, and it had been a gift from the provincial government. There was no public art gallery, and it was only through the hobby of a resident oil millionaire, Eric Harvie, that the nucleus of a substantial museum and archives was established. Given this poor record, the Heritage Park movement of the mid 1960s, sponsored in part by the City of Calgary, represented a change in philosophy and a new civic awareness of the need to preserve tangible links with the past.

Calgary's society in 1965 was young, and the many newly arrived married couples were more concerned with raising young families than with opportunities for cultural expression or social activity. For them, Calgary provided the necessary ingredients of a satisfying urban life. And while the city did not possess the cultural sophistication of Montreal or Toronto, it also did not face spiralling crime rates or social disequilibrium. The Calgary of 1965 provided most of its residents with a good urban life free from many of the usual difficulties of social unrest and congestion. As a city in transition, it had not yet moved into the stage where further growth had to be measured in terms of the problems it created.

For a city with such a strong western tradition, there was little visible evidence of the past in the Calgary of 1965. Old buildings fell under the demolition hammer, sometimes faster than the dedicated photographer could preserve them for antiquity. The site of the original Fort Calgary lay buried under weeds, creosoted trackage and a warehouse. Calgary's newness stood in sharp contrast to the few areas where multiple land use had not defiled the dignity of age. In the leafy areas of east Calgary away from the stores and the traffic, in sections of old Mount Royal among the stone walls and out of view of the apartments or even in the crumbling serenity of Sunnyside, it is still possible to resurrect visually those days that otherwise exist only in books, photographs or dimming memories.

For in 1965 modern Calgary was on the move. The long-held vision of bigness was coming to fruition in a frenzy of expansion. There were not many among such a young population who had grown with the city and had noticed the change. Only a handful could remember what Calgary was like in the 1920s. On the benches in Central Park opposite where Pat Burns used to live, old-timers sat in the sun with their memories. Probably there were some among them who could recall the days before the streetcars, when cattle still used the Macleod Trail and the railway stretched its lonely length along Ninth Avenue west to the mountains. But even the recent years are the distant past to those who cannot remember.

Aerial view of Calgary, September 1959. The oil industry has had a dramatic impact on Calgary's urban landscape. Since 1945, the city's downtown core has been almost entirely rebuilt. The sandstone structures of the pre-1914 period have been replaced by towering skyscrapers that house Shell, Gulf, Texaco and similar companies. The CPR, one of the city's first corporate citizens, has also contributed to this physical change. Rising from the CPR's immensely valuable core property is the 600-foot Calgary Tower, which stands as the centrepiece of a sizeable commercial development.

Calgary, July 1978

Appendix
Statistical Tables

TABLE I
The Growth of Manufacturing in Calgary, 1891-1971

Year	Population	Number of Firms*	Number of Employees	Payroll $(000)	Value of Products $(000)
1891	3,876	28	169	97	259
1901	4,398	10	307	175	599
1911	43,704	46	2,133	1,570	7,751
1921	63,305	149	2,516	3,783	19,879
1931	83,761	155	4,502	5,644	28,000
1941	88,904	207	5,239	7,291	49,869
1951	129,060	309	8,658	22,905	152,277
1961	249,641	367	9,717	41,928	253,182
1971	403,319	546	10,892	77,276	576,878

*The discrepancy between 1891 and 1901 is accounted for by the fact that the 1891 figure includes *all* establishments, regardless of size, while the figures for 1901-1971 are based on firms with *five or more* employees.

Source: *Censuses of Canada, 1891-1971; The Manufacturing Industries of Canada, 1941;* and *Canada Year Books, 1924, 1954, 1965* and *1974.*

TABLE II
Number of Males Per 1,000 Females in Calgary, 1891-1971

Year	Number of Males	Number of Females	Ratio
1891	2,151	1,725	1247.0
1901	2,437	1,955	1246.5
1911	26,565	17,139	1550.0
1921	31,828	31,479	1010.0
1931	43,345	40,416	1072.5
1941	45,543	44,361	1004.1
1951	63,379	65,081	983.1
1961	125,304	124,337	1007.7
1971	201,024	202,295	993.0

Source: *Censuses of Canada, 1891-1971.*

TABLE III
Population Growth in Calgary,
1891-1971

Year	Population	Numerical Change	Per Cent Change
1891	3,876	—	—
1901	4,398	522	13.5
1906	11,967	7,569	172.5
1911	43,704	31,737	265.2
1916	56,514	12,810	29.3
1921	63,305	6,791	12.0
1926	65,291	1,986	3.1
1931	83,761	18,470	28.3
1936	83,407	−354	−.4
1941	88,904	5,497	6.6
1946	100,044	11,140	12.5
1951	129,060	29,016	29.0
1956	181,780	52,720	40.8
1961	249,641	67,861	37.3
1966	330,575	80,934	32.4
1971	403,319	72,744	22.0

Source: *Censuses of Canada, 1891-1971; Censuses of the Prairie Provinces, 1916-1946.*

TABLE IV

Population Growth in the Calgary Metropolitan Area, 1891-1971

Year	Population of Core	Population of Suburbs	Total Population of the Metropolitan Area	Numerical Change	Per Cent Change
1891	3,876	—	3,876	—	—
1901	4,398	—	4,398	522	13.5
1911	43,704	—	43,704	39,306	893.7
1921	63,305	—	63,305	19,601	44.8
1931	83,761	—	83,761	20,456	32.3
1941	88,904	5,096	94,000	10,239	12.2
1951	129,060	12,158	141,218	47,218	33.4
1961	249,641	29,421	279,062	137,844	97.6
1971	403,319	*	403,319	124,257	44.5

*In 1961 and 1964, the Calgary city limits were extended to include all of the suburbs and fringe areas.

Source: *Censuses of Canada, 1891-1971; Calgary Municipal Manuals, 1965* and *1974*; and *Metropolitan Calgary Population: Historical Review, 1946-1970*.

TABLE V

Birthplace of Calgary's Canadian-Born Population, 1911-1961

Birthplace	1911		1921		1931		1941		1951		1961	
	No.	%	No.	%	No.	%	No.	%	No.	%	No.	%
Maritimes*	2,173	5.0	2,570	4.0	2,650	3.2	2,346	2.6	3,237	2.5	5,486	2.2
Quebec	1,174	2.7	1,364	2.1	1,364	1.6	1,247	1.4	1,799	1.4	2,985	1.1
Ontario	9,868	22.5	10,142	16.0	9,949	11.9	8,533	9.6	10,615	8.2	15,534	6.2
Manitoba	731	1.7	1,355	2.1	2,619	3.1	3,274	3.7	5,779	4.5	11,571	4.6
Saskatchewan	183	0.4	737	1.1	1,864	2.2	3,852	4.3	11,053	8.6	24,425	9.8
Alberta	4,658	10.6	16,126	25.5	26,624	31.8	36,766	41.3	57,161	44.3	118,492	47.5
British Columbia	201	0.4	322	0.5	1,281	1.5	1,667	1.8	3,440	2.7	8,310	3.3
Yukon and Territories	5	.01	1	.0	4	.0	12	.0	32	.0	167	.1
Not Given	203	0.4	67	.1	72	.1	8	.0	—	—	—	—
Total Canadian-Born	19,296	44.1	32,684	52.4	46,427	53.9	57,705	65.6	93,116	75.4	186,970	77.3
Total Population	43,704	100	63,305	100	83,761	100	88,904	100	129,060	100	249,641	100

*Includes Newfoundland in 1951 and 1961.
Source: *Censuses of Canada, 1911-1961*.

TABLE VI

Birthplace of Calgary's Foreign-Born Population, 1911-1961

Birthplace	1911		1921		1931		1941		1951		1961	
	No.	%	No.	%	No.	%	No.	%	No.	%	No.	%
Great Britain	15,474	35.4	20,918	33.0	23,640	28.2	19,507	21.9	19,144	14.8	23,442	9.4
United States	3,111	7.1	5,060	8.0	5,430	6.5	4,934	5.5	6,652	5.1	9,446	3.8
Scandinavia	709	1.6	477	0.7	1,629	1.9	951	1.1	1,442	1.1	2,828	1.1
Germany	3,584	8.2	354	0.6	664	0.8	452	0.5	427	0.3	5,525	2.2
Italy	369	0.8	255	0.4	276	0.3	254	0.3	412	0.3	2,636	1.0
France	84	0.2	138	0.2	136	0.2	116	0.1	—	—	—	—
Other European	550	1.2	2,088	3.3	5,722	6.8	3,667	4.1	—	—	—	—
Asian	542	1.2	677	1.1	993	1.2	657	0.7	775	0.6	1,754	0.7
Others and Unspecified	105	0.2	173	0.3	164	0.2	186	0.2	3,181	2.5	11,156	4.5
Total Foreign-Born	24,528	55.9	29,240	47.6	38,654	46.1	30,724	34.4	32,033	24.6	56,787	22.7
Total Population	43,704	100	63,305	100	83,761	100	88,904	100	129,060	100	249,641	100

Source: *Censuses of Canada, 1911-1961*.

TABLE VII

Ethnic Origins of Calgary's Population, 1901-1961

Ethnic Group	1901 No.	1901 %	1911 No.	1911 %	1921 No.	1921 %	1931 No.	1931 %	1941 No.	1941 %	1951 No.	1951 %	1961 No.	1961 %
Asian	64	2.6	56	0.1	729	1.2	1,136	1.4	849	0.9	1,110	0.8	2,688	1.0
British	3,578	80.2	30,884	71.3	52,206	82.4	64,400	76.4	67,846	76.3	88,416	68.5	147,030	58.9
French	125	3.0	705	1.6	1,428	2.2	1,755	2.0	2,279	2.6	4,012	3.1	9,528	3.8
German	197	4.8	2,608	6.0	876	1.4	3,751	4.5	3,014	3.3	8,794	6.8	26,917	10.8
Italian	—	—	114	0.3	425	0.7	620	0.7	661	0.7	1,091	0.8	4,720	1.9
Dutch	23	0.6	348	0.8	628	1.0	1,035	1.3	1,559	1.7	2,528	2.0	8,682	3.5
Scandinavian	195	4.8	977	2.2	1,395	2.3	3,413	4.0	3,757	4.3	6,631	5.2	4,493	1.8
Russian*	64	1.6	485	1.1	1,973	3.1	1,028	1.2	2,315	2.6	1,981	1.5	3,584	1.4
Ukrainian	—	—	—	—	153	0.2	807	1.0	959	1.0	3,033	2.4	7,075	2.8
Polish	—	—	928	2.1	287	0.5	807	1.0	1,310	1.5	2,151	1.6	5,106	2.0
Jewish	—	—	369	0.8	1,247	2.0	1,622	1.9	1,794	2.0	1,713	1.3	1,856	0.7
Native Peoples	101	2.3	878	2.0	22	—	8	—	14	—	62	—	335	0.1
Others and Unspecified	51	1.1	6,152	11.7	1,936	3.0	3,779	4.6	2,547	3.1	7,538	6.0	27,627	11.3
Total	4,398	100	43,704	100	63,305	100	83,761	100	88,904	100	129,060	100	249,641	100

*Russian includes the following: 1901 – Austro-Hungarian; 1911 – Austrian, Hungarian, Bulgarian and Romanian; 1921, 1931, 1941 – Austrian, Czech, Slovak, Hungarian and Romanian; 1951 – Austrian, Czech, Slovak and Hungarian; 1961 – U.S.S.R.

Source: *Censuses of Canada, 1901-1961.*

TABLE VIII

Major Religious Affiliations of Calgary's Population, 1901-1961

Religion	1901 No.	1901 %	1911 No.	1911 %	1921 No.	1921 %	1931 No.	1931 %	1941 No.	1941 %	1951 No.	1951 %	1961 No.	1961 %
Anglican	1,253	25.4	10,124	23.1	18,036	28.4	22,296	26.6	22,249	25.0	27,341	21.2	42,591	17.1
Baptist	343	6.9	2,769	6.3	4,013	6.3	5,505	6.6	5,907	6.6	6,800	5.3	10,208	4.1
Methodist*	941	19.1	8,240	18.8	10,008	15.8	22,153	26.4	24,026	27.0	44,942	34.8	87,258	34.9
Presbyterian	1,305	26.5	10,378	23.7	17,112	27.0	12,664	15.1	12,700	14.3	11,733	9.1	14,524	5.8
Lutheran	388	7.8	2,399	5.5	2,382	3.8	4,631	5.5	4,584	5.2	7,045	5.5	18,195	7.3
Jewish	7	—	613	1.4	1,233	1.9	1,604	1.9	1,760	2.0	2,094	1.6	2,866	1.1
Roman Catholic	537	10.9	4,183	9.6	6,376	10.1	10,571	12.6	10,406	11.7	17,639	13.7	48,121	19.3
Buddhist and Confucian	—	—	229	0.5	498	0.8	461	0.5	478	0.5	189	0.1	301	0.1
Other and No Religion	150	3.4	4,769	11.1	3,647	5.9	3,876	4.8	6,794	7.7	11,278	8.7	25,577	10.3
Total	4,924	100	43,704	100	63,308	100	83,761	100	88,904	100	129,060	100	249,641	100

*Becomes the United Church in 1925 and includes Congregationalists and some Presbyterians after that date.

Source: *Censuses of Canada, 1901-1961.*

TABLE IX
Age Composition of Calgary's Population, 1921-1961

Year	0–14		15–44		45–64		65+		Total Population
	No.	%	No.	%	No.	%	No.	%	
1921	19,883	31.4	33,185	52.4	8,806	13.9	1,349	2.1	63,305
1931	22,302	26.6	43,085	51.4	16,631	19.8	3,036	3.6	83,761
1941	19,510	21.9	44,011	49.5	20,703	23.3	5,680	6.4	88,904
1951	30,456	23.6	61,664	47.8	24,916	19.3	12,024	9.3	129,060
1961	81,121	32.5	111,701	44.7	38,428	15.4	18,391	7.4	249,641

Source: *Censuses of Canada, 1921-1961.*

TABLE X
Crude Oil and Natural Gas Production in Alberta, 1947-1972

Year	Crude Oil (barrels)	Per Cent of National Production	Value of Production $(000)	Gas (mcf)	Per Cent of National Production	Value of Producers' Sales $(000)
To 1947	75,793,679	69.2	—	1,677,953,812	78.5	—
1952	58,836,653	96.2	139,658	91,380,217	90.3	5,936
1957	136,766,453	75.5	358,554	223,284,148	79.7	13,735
1962	165,187,031	67.6	388,483	783,359,503	79.1	78,869
1967	230,482,518	65.8	588,771	1,250,948,402	79.8	150,562
1972	424,431,230	78.3	1,210,465	2,457,630,710	81.8	307,471

Source: *Alberta Industry and Resources, 1975,* Tables 33, 34; *Canadian Petroleum Association Statistical Year Book, 1972,* p. 64.

TABLE XI
Building Permits Issued
in Calgary, 1907-1968

Year	Number	Value in Millions of Dollars*
1907	605	—
1908	423	—
1909	777	—
1910	1,499	—
1911	2,619	5.5
1912	3,843	20.4
1913	2,078	—
1920	870	2.8
1925	772	1.2
1929	1,883	11.4
1930	1,545	4.0
1940	1,523	2.7
1945	2,448	7.2
1950	4,136	25.8
1953	4,972	42.1
1955	5,515	58.9
1958	7,278	101.6
1960	5,846	99.3
1961	6,491	70.4
1962	6,421	88.0
1963	5,659	91.2
1964	5,715	95.1
1965	5,952	129.1
1966	5,784	114.4
1967	6,644	136.9
1968	8,004	183.1

*Figures are not available for 1907, 1908, 1909, 1910 and 1913.
Source: *Calgary Municipal Manuals, 1974* and *1975-1976*.

TABLE XII
The Labour Force of Calgary by Industry, 1911-1961

Industry	1911	1921	1951	1961
Primary: agriculture, forestry, fishing, trapping & mining	4.2	4.3	1.6	1.4
Manufacturing	15.1	14.1	17.2	12.0
Construction	20.8	7.6	9.7	9.7
Transportation	12.6	14.5	7.2	11.2
Trade & Commerce	21.8	19.1	19.2	21.8
Service	19.2	29.8	27.9	30.4
Other or unspecified	6.3	10.6	17.2	13.5
	100%	100%	100%	100%

Source: *Censuses of Canada, 1911-1961.*

Notes

INTRODUCTION

[1]The North West Mounted Police came into being through a Privy Council order passed August 30, 1873. As Mounted Police historian S.W. Horrall points out, it was a "legally constituted body to maintain law and order on the western prairies". After recruitment during the winter of 1873-74, the march west began from Fort Dufferin on July 8, 1874 with an original force of 275 men. The site of present-day Fort Macleod was reached towards the end of the second week in October. For a good account of these events, see S.W. Horrall, "The March West," in H. Dempsey, ed., *Men in Scarlet* (Calgary, 1974), pp.14-26.

[2]The whisky trade activity is discussed in L.H. Bussard, "Early History of Calgary," unpublished M.A. thesis, University of Alberta, 1935, pp. 11-13.

[3]Hugh Dempsey, unpublished article, undated and untitled, in possession of author.

[4]For additional information on Brisebois, see Hugh A. Dempsey, "Brisebois: Calgary's Forgotten Founder," in A.W. Rasporich and Henry Klassen, eds., *Frontier Calgary: Town, City and Region, 1875-1914* (Calgary, 1975), pp. 28-40.

[5]George Stanley, "The Naming of Calgary," *Alberta History*, Vol. 23, No. 3 (Summer 1975), pp. 7-9.

[6]L.V. Kelly, *The Rangemen* (Toronto, 1913), pp. 156, 164.

[7]Bussard, "Early History," pp. 34-35.

[8]J. Egan to William Van Horne, August 1, 1883. Copy of correspondence in possession of author.

[9]Bussard, "Early History," p. 52.

[10]*Ibid.*, pp. 50-51.

[11]*Regina Leader*, July 19, 1883; and *Calgary Herald*, January 30, 1884.

[12]See M.L. Foran, "Early Calgary, 1875-1895: The Controversy Surrounding the Townsite Location and the Direction of Town Expansion," in A.R. McCormack and Ian MacPherson, eds., *Cities in the West: Papers of the Western Canada Urban History Conference* (Ottawa, 1975), pp. 26-45.

[13]C.P. Brydges to L. Russell, October 18, 1882, Dominion Lands Correspondence, Public Archives of Canada, Ottawa.

[14]Wesley Orr to J.J.C. Abbott, May 27, 1889, Wesley Orr Papers, Historical Library and Archives, Glenbow-Alberta Institute, Calgary.

[15]*Calgary Herald*, October 15, 1884; and *Calgary Tribune*, September 11, 1886.

[16]George Murdoch diary, June 25, 1885, George Murdoch Papers, Glenbow-Alberta Institute.

[17]See E. Hanson, *Local Government in Alberta* (Toronto, 1965), pp. 8-9.

CHAPTER ONE

[1]*Calgary Herald*, March 21, 1884.

[2]*Calgary Tribune*, December 19, 1888; and February 3, 1892.

[3]Wesley Orr to Carling, March 1, 1892, Wesley Orr Papers, Glenbow-Alberta Institute.

[4]Calgary Brewing and Malting Company Papers, Box 61, Folder 486, Glenbow-Alberta Institute.

[5]*Calgary Herald*, February 17, 1892.

[6]T. Ward, *Cowtown: An Album of Early Calgary* (Calgary, 1975), p.198.

[7]*Calgary Tribune*, December 1886.

[8]For a discussion of these factors, see Kelly, *The Rangemen*; and S. Evans, "The Passing of a Frontier: Ranching in the Canadian West, 1882-1912," unpublished Ph.D. dissertation, University of Calgary, 1976.

[9]See A.F. Sproule, "The Role of Patrick Burns in the Development of Western Canada," unpublished M.A. thesis, University of Alberta, 1962.

[10]*Calgary News Telegram*, March 25, 1912.

[11]Sproule, "Role of Patrick Burns," p. 92.

[12]*North-West Territories Gazette*, April 1891.

[13]R. Cunniffe, *Calgary in Sandstone* (Calgary, 1969), p. 3.

[14]E. Roper, *By Track and Trails Through Canada* (London, 1891), p. 375.

[15]Calgary Council Minutes, June 23, 1889.

[16]See M.L. Foran, "The Calgary Town Council, 1884-1895: A Study of

Local Government in a Frontier Environment," unpublished M.A. thesis, University of Calgary, 1970, pp. 116, 119.

[17]Calgary Council Minutes, April 1, 1895.

[18]A copy of this pamphlet is in the Glenbow-Alberta Institute collection.

[19]See E.A. Mitchner, "William Pearce, 1882-1904," unpublished Ph.D. dissertation, University of Alberta, 1971.

[20]See M.L. Foran, "Urban Calgary, 1884-1895," *Histoire sociale/Social History*, Vol. V, No. 9 (April 1972), pp. 66-67.

[21]*Calgary Tribune*, March 7, 1888.

[22]City of Calgary Voters Lists 1894, 1895, Glenbow-Alberta Institute.

[23]G. MacInnes, *In the Shadow of the Rockies* (London, 1930), pp. 329-330.

[24]See H. Klassen, "The *Bond of Brotherhood* and Calgary Workingmen," in Rasporich and Klassen, eds., *Frontier Calgary*, pp. 267-271.

[25]*Calgary Herald*, March 16, 1892.

[26]*Bond of Brotherhood*, November 28, 1903.

[27]Wesley Orr to R. Elliott, Wesley Orr Papers, Glenbow-Alberta Institute.

[28]See M.L. Foran, "Land Speculation and Urban Development: Calgary, 1884-1912," in Rasporich and Klassen, eds., *Frontier Calgary*, pp. 203-220.

[29]Chinese laundries were singled out because potential health hazards were created by the disposal of waste waters into holes beneath the floors of the laundries.

[30]*Calgary Herald*, August 5, 1892.

[31]Record Group 18, B1, Vol. 1255, File 356, Public Archives of Canada.

[32]*Calgary Herald*, August 24, 1892.

[33]See *Calgary Herald*, May 28, 1884; January 8 and March 5, 1885; March 6 and August 14, 1889.

[34]*Calgary Herald*, March 5, 1885.

[35]Century Calgary Publications, *At Your Service Part II* (Calgary, 1975), pp. 26-27.

[36]See Foran, "Early Calgary".

[37]See *Calgary Herald*, July 24 and August 20, 1890; and *Calgary Tribune*, September 20, 1890.

[38]See *Calgary Tribune*, July 31, November 19 and December 3, 1886; and Calgary Council Minutes, May 1887.

[39]See Foran, "Early Calgary".

[40]*Calgary Tribune*, December 18, 1889.

[41]*The Western World*, August 1890, p. 143.

[42]See Foran, "Calgary Town Council," pp. 117-118.

[43]See *Calgary Herald*, December 5 and 19, 1888; May 18, 1889; February 7 and 14, 1894; August 7, 1895.

[44]A.E. Cross Papers, Box 56, No. 448, Glenbow-Alberta Institute. See also Foran, "Calgary Town Council," pp. 76-77.

[45]See *Calgary Herald*, May 29, 1893; and *Calgary Tribune*, June 4, 1895.

[46]See Ward, *Cowtown*, p. 316.

[47]A Calgary Liberal Party Association was not formed until 1891. See *Calgary Herald*, April 22, 1891.

[48]See *Calgary Tribune*, October 21, 1885 and April 3, 1886.

[49]The most colourful and controversial manifestation of group action occurred in 1885-1886 and concerned Judge Jeremiah Travis and the liquor law. See M.L. Foran, "The Travis Affair and the Town of Calgary, 1885-1886," *Alberta Historical Review*, Vol. 19 (Autumn 1971), pp. 1-7.

[50]See D. Coats, "Calgary: The Private Schools, 1910-1916," in Rasporich and Klassen, eds., *Frontier Calgary*, pp. 140-152.

[51]See Foran, "Urban Calgary," p. 74.

[52]For a good discussion of education in Calgary, see R.M. Stamp, *School Days: A Century of Memories* (Calgary, 1975).

[53]*Calgary Tribune*, January 6 and June 8 and 15, 1892.

[54]*Ibid.*, February 7, 1894.

[55]*Ibid.*, October 12, 1892; and *Calgary Herald*, April 4, 1892.

CHAPTER TWO

[1]*Calgary Herald*, July 18, 1908.

[2]*Census of Canada 1931*, Vol. VIII.

[3]*Calgary Herald*, December 20, 1916.

[4]Calgary Board of Trade, "Calgary, the Inter-Western Pacific Railway Centre," 1908, Calgary Brewing and Malting Company Papers, Box 61, File folder 486, Glenbow-Alberta Institute.

[5]See *The 100,000 Manufacturing Building and Wholesale Book Edition*, published by the *Calgary Albertan*, 1914.

[6]*High River Times*, May 18, 1911.

[7]See *The 100,000 Manufacturing*.

[8]*Census of Canada 1911*, Vol. III. The increase was from $599,000 to over $11 million.

[9]See L.P. Strong, "The Handling of Western Grain," *Prosperous Canada*, published by the *Calgary Herald*, 1909.

[10]*High River Times*, March 4, 1909.

[11]*Calgary Herald*, September 15, 1917.

[12]*Ibid*.

[13]Kelly, *The Rangemen*, p. 431.

[14]Calgary Board of Trade, *Annual Report 1908*.

[15]*Census of Canada 1911*, Vol. VI, pp. 342-350.

[16]*St. Francis Bulletin* (California), February 12, 1913.

[17]*The 100,000 Manufacturing*.

[18]*Calgary Herald*, May 21, 1907.

[19]*Ibid.*, October 20, 1916.

[20]*Calgary Optimist*, December 11, 1909.

[21]For information about Dick and Crandell, see A.O. MacRae, *History of the Province of Alberta*, Vol. II (Calgary, 1912), pp. 639, 943-944.

[22]See Foran, "Land Speculation," pp. 214-215.

[23]Some of Calgary's most prominent real estate men included Adoniran J. Samis, Malcolm Daniel Geddes, William Arthur Lowry, William Toole and Bert A. Stringer. For information about these men and others, see MacRae, *History of Alberta*, Vol. I, pp. 554, 873, 1014; and Vol. II, pp. 622, 927, 944.

[24]A newspaper clipping file on Freddie Lowes is included in the Glenbow-Alberta Institute collection.

[25]Calgary Council Minutes, July 7, 1911.

[26]*Ibid.*, July 19, 1910.

[27]See, for example, *Calgary Tribune*, June 12, 1889.

[28]*The 100,000 Manufacturing*, p. 127.

[29]*Calgary Herald*, November 1, 1916.

[30]*Ibid.*, November 27, 1914.

[31]*Ibid.*, May 9, 1908.

[32]*Calgary Optimist*, December 11, 1909.

[33]*Calgary Herald*, November 14, 1914.

[34]See MacRae, *History of Alberta*, Vol. I, p. 565.

[35]Evans, "The Passing of a Frontier," pp. 376-377.

[36]For a discussion of the Chinese population, see G.A. Baureiss, "The City and the Sub-Community: The Chinese of Calgary," unpublished M.A. thesis, University of Calgary, 1971; and J. Brian Dawson, "The Chinese Experience in Frontier Calgary, 1885-1910," in Rasporich and Klassen, eds., *Frontier Calgary*.

[37]For examples, see *Calgary Herald*, August 13 and 19, 1909; September 13, 1910.

[38]City Planning Commission of Calgary, "Report of Town Planner, Thomas Mawson," in *The City of Calgary Past, Present and Future* (Calgary, 1914), pp. 50-51.

[39]See *News Telegram*, March 27, 1912.

[40]*Financial World*, July 20, 1912.

[41]*The 100,000 Manufacturing*, p. 126.

[42]Calgary Council Minutes, June 9, 1913; and *Calgary Herald*, November 24, 1914.

[43]City of Calgary, City Clerk Files, Box 11.

[44]*Calgary Herald*, December 15, 1916.

[45]The candidate was R.J. Tallon, president of the machinists union. See *Calgary Herald*, November 20, 1914; November 27, 1915.

[46]For a good discussion of the Calgary labour movement during this period, see E.A. Taraska, "The Calgary Craft Union Movement, 1900-1920," unpublished M.A. thesis, University of Calgary, 1975.

[47]*Ibid.*, p. 8.

[48]*Labour Gazette*, July 1911.

[49]Taraska, "Calgary Craft Union," p. 35.

[50]See *Calgary Herald*, September 2, 1911.

[51]The plebiscite calling for the abolition of the ward system apparently recognized only that the wards *then in existence* were unsatisfactory. The ward system was one of many issues voted on at the time, and it is likely that public interest was less than it would have been if the ward question had been the only question on the ballot.

[52]These issues are discussed in D.H. Breen, "The Canadian West and the Ranching Frontier, 1875-1922," unpublished Ph.D. dissertation, University of Alberta, 1972.

[53]For a good discussion of this topic, see D. Smith, "Liberals and Conservatives on the Prairies, 1917-1968," in D. Gagan, ed., *Prairie Perspectives: Papers of the Western Canadian Studies Conference* (Toronto, 1970), pp. 30-43.

[54]Quoted in *Calgary Albertan*, March 8, 1956.

[55]*Ibid.*

[56]See Stamp, *School Days*.

[57]*Calgary Herald*, July 3, 1909.

[58]See "Calgary, 'Temple of Knowledge': A History of the Public Library," in *At Your Service Part I*, pp. 4-5.

[59]*Calgary Herald*, April 20, 1909; March 5, 1912.

[60]*The 100,000 Manufacturing*.

[61]For a biography of Bob Edwards, see J.W. Grant MacEwan, *Eye Opener Bob* (Edmonton, 1957).

[62]*Eye Opener*, October 25, 1911.

[63]*Ibid.*, April 10, 1920.

[64]*Ibid.*, December 7, 1918; April 8 and July 8, 1916.

CHAPTER THREE

[1]For a discussion of western Canadian grain farming, see J.W. Grant MacEwan, *Harvest of Bread* (Saskatoon, 1969).

[2]*Census of the Prairie Provinces 1946*.

[3]MacEwan, *Harvest*, p. 119.

[4]F.M. Baker, "The Meat Packer and the Cattle Industry," *Canadian Cattlemen* (June 1938), p. 44.

[5]C.W. Vrooman, "Cattle Price Fluctuations," *Canadian Cattlemen* (March 1942), p. 157.

[6]C.A. Lyndon, "An Economic Survey of the Livestock Industry of Alberta," *Canadian Cattlemen* (December 1938), p. 114.

[7]F.M. Baker, "Packing House Facilities and Practices," *Canadian Cattlemen* (December 1938), p. 107.

[8]See P.N.R. Morrison and E.C. Morrison, *The Story of Calgary* (Calgary, 1950).

[9]See W.H.S. Boote, *Ogden Whistle* (Calgary, 1975).

[10]Calgary Board of Trade, *Annual Report 1928*.

[11]See J.C. Sproule, "Exploration and Discovery," in James Hilborn, ed., *Dusters and Gushers* (Toronto, 1968).

[12]A.W. Dingman and C. Dingman Papers, Box 1, File folder 7, Glenbow-Alberta Institute.

[13]*Calgary Herald*, October 16, 1914.

[14]*Ibid.*, November 15, 1916.

[15]James Gray, *The Roar of the Twenties* (Toronto, 1975), pp. 311-336.

[16]*Calgary Herald*, July 6, 1929.

[17]G.H. Zieber, "Calgary as an Oil Administrative and Oil Operations Centre," in B.M. Barr, ed., *Calgary: Metropolitan Structure and Influence*, Western Geographical Series, Vol. 11 (Victoria, 1975), p. 78.

[18]See G. Lonn, "Canadian Oil Pioneers," in Hilborn, ed., *Dusters and Gushers*.

[19]For the statistics in this paragraph, see P.J. Smith, *Study of Calgary's Past and Probable Future Population Growth* (Calgary, 1959), pp. 6-7, 12, 17.

[20]For the statistics in this paragraph, see *Census of the Prairie Provinces 1946*, Vol. I, Table 5; and Vol. III, Table 21.

[21]Brasso and Weismose are discussed in Morrison and Morrison, *Story of Calgary*.

[22]*Calgary Herald*, April 2 and May 28, 1942.

[23]Calgary Council Minutes, April 10, 1942.

[24]*Census of Canada 1931*.

[25]For the statistics in this paragraph, see *Census of the Prairie Provinces 1946*.

[26]Calgary Council Minutes, March 30, 1925.

[27]This statement is probably not quite accurate. Statistics show that over 17 million passengers used streetcars in 1929. When divided by the population, this figure equals 50 per cent. However, most passengers would be using the cars on a return trip basis.

[28]Specific provisions were contained in Bylaw 763. See, for example, City of Calgary, City Clerk Files, Box 590.

[29]*Census of the Prairie Provinces 1946*, Vol. III, Table 10.

[30]For the statistics in this paragraph, see "Financial Statement of the City of Calgary 1914," Glenbow-Alberta Institute; *Calgary Herald*, September 3, 1915; Calgary Board of Trade, *Annual Report 1933*; and Calgary Council Minutes, July 23, 1941.

[31]Calgary Council, "Report of the Special Housing Committee of City Council," July 19, 1929.

[32]For the statistics in this paragraph, see Calgary Council Minutes, February 26 and October 23, 1941; June 30 and August 27, 1943; April 26 and July 18, 1944; February 19, March 3 and April 16, 1945; June 5 and October 22, 1946.

[33]Thomas Underwood Papers 1904-48, Box 5, File folder 46, January 19, 1944, Glenbow-Alberta Institute.

[34]Statistics indicating Calgary's financial difficulties are found in City of Calgary, City Clerk Files, Boxes 132, 166.

[35]See W.R. Rolph, *Henry Wise Wood of Alberta* (Toronto, 1950).

[36]*Ibid.*, p. 79.

[37]*Ibid.*, p. 138.

[38]The Aberhart phenomenon is documented in many excellent studies. See, for example, L.P.V. Johnson and Ola MacNutt, *Aberhart of Alberta* (Edmonton, 1970); and David R. Elliott, "Antithetical Elements in William Aberhart's Theology and Political Ideology," *Canadian Historical Review*, Vol. LIX, No. 1 (March 1978), pp. 38-58.

[39]Thomas Underwood, long-time Conservative businessman, wrote in 1938: "We have an extraordinary government and we will have to put up with it for another two years anyway, and what will be the end of it is hard to say." For this and related statements, see T. Underwood Papers, Box 5, File folders 45, 46, Glenbow-Alberta Institute.

CHAPTER FOUR

[1]See Alberta Department of Business Development and Tourism, *Industries and Resources 1975*, Table 4, Table 17; and *Canadian Petroleum Association Statistical Year Book 1972*, p. 64.

[2]See Zieber, "Calgary as an Oil Centre".

[3]See *Oilweek*, May 16, 1966, p. 25; March 3, 1969, pp. 44-46; March 16, 1970.

[4]See J. Wood, "Housing in the North," *Proceedings of the Petroleum Aluminum Industry Arctic Exchange Meeting* (Calgary, 1970).

[5]Zieber, "Calgary as an Oil Centre," p. 83.

[6]See B.M. Barr, "The Importance of Regional Inter-Industry Linkages to Calgary's Manufacturing Firms," in Barr, ed., *Calgary: Metropolitan Structure and Influence*.

[7]See Alberta Department of Business Development and Tourism, *Industries and Resources 1975*, Table 78, Table 85; and Smith, *Study of Calgary's Population Growth*, p. 25.

[8]For the statistics used in this paragraph, see Government of Alberta and University of Alberta, *Atlas of Alberta* (Edmonton, 1969), p.54.

[9]See P.J. Smith and D.G. Harasym, "Planning for Retail Services in New Residential Areas Since 1944," in Barr, ed., *Calgary: Metropolitan Structure and Influence*, pp. 113, 176-178.

[10]This trend did not really begin until the late 1960s.

[11]Alberta Department of Business Development and Tourism, *Industries and Resources 1975*, Table 41.

[12]See P.J. Smith, "Edmonton and Calgary: Growing Together," *Canadian Geographic Journal* (May-June 1976), pp. 26-33.

[13]As a postscript, it should be noted that by 1971, with Manning no longer a factor, an urban-based party led by young, aggressive city politicians had tumbled Social Credit from office. Like its predecessor, the victorious Conservative Party was Calgary-inspired and once more vindicated the city's role as a moulder of political alternatives at the provincial level.

Suggestions for Further Reading

There is not a great deal of published literature relating to the history of Calgary. Only recently has there been an increase in the number of academic studies on various aspects of the city's development. Most are M.A. theses and Ph.D. dissertations, and almost all are unpublished. However, these studies are available in some form or other in most university libraries. There has been no formal study of the city, except for the brief summary of development contained in George Nader's *Cities of Canada, Volume Two: Profiles of Fifteen Metropolitan Centres* (Toronto: Macmillan of Canada, 1976). The papers presented at the University of Calgary's conference on the city's history have been assembled in A.W. Rasporich and Henry Klassen, eds., *Frontier Calgary: Town, City and Region, 1875-1914* (Calgary: University of Calgary and McClelland and Stewart West, 1975). This is the most comprehensive historical study of Calgary to date. For a detailed listing of material on Calgary, see Alan F.J. Artibise, *Western Canada Since 1870: A Select Bibliography and Guide* (Vancouver: University of British Columbia Press, 1978).

Calgary is fortunate in possessing excellent archival resources. The Historical Library and Archives of the Glenbow-Alberta Institute houses an abundance of primary and secondary materials on Calgary, which are essential to any in-depth study of the city. See S.S. Jameson, "The Archives of the Glenbow-Alberta Institute (Calgary)," *Urban History Review*, No. 3-77 (February 1978), pp. 69-79. The City of Calgary Planning Department also has an up-to-date library containing contemporary material on urban development. Almost every study undertaken by the city over the past 20 years is available on request, as well as comparative material on Canadian and American cities.

In the preparation of this volume the author relied to a marked degree on primary documents, and the following source listing includes some of the most important of these. Generally, however, the reader will be directed to those secondary sources that supplement and expand upon themes treated in this book.

GENERAL SOURCES

Histories of Calgary do exist. Indeed, they are generally very readable and provide illuminating insights into past events and personalities. Two have appeared since centennial year. *Calgary: A Not Too Solemn Look at Calgary's First 100 Years* (Calgary: The Calgary Herald, 1974) was prepared by *Herald* staff writer Bob Shiels as part of that newspaper's centenary project. Tom Ward, a long-time resident of the city and a former employee of the Public Information Department of the City of Calgary, has written *Cowtown: An Album of Early Calgary* (Calgary: McClelland and Stewart West, 1975), which covers the 1876-1914 period. Both Shiels and Ward have used photographs extensively and to good purpose.

Leishmann McNeill, son of a pioneer, reminisced in a series of articles entitled *Tales of the Old Town* (Calgary: The Calgary Herald, u.d.). Some very good anecdotal material is contained in this small book. Probably the best-known of the popular histories is Grant MacEwan's *Calgary Cavalcade* (Edmonton: Institute of Applied Art, 1958). The Century Calgary Society has produced 32 studies in six volumes which appear under the general title, *Century Calgary Publications*. These amateur studies cover a wide range of topics relative to the city's history and contain a wealth of factual information. Two excellent photographic collections by Trudy Soby form part of this series; these 1975 volumes, entitled *A Walk Through Old Calgary* and *Be It Ever So Humble*, are worth examining. Mention should also be made of the impressive slide collection of Allison Jackson, an amateur photographer and former librarian who has assembled and catalogued a vast array of pertinent information to accompany every slide on various Calgary landmarks.

Calgary's contemporary metropolitan role and its internal socio-economic structure are discussed in a recent volume edited by Brenton M. Barr and entitled *Calgary: Metropolitan Structure and Influence*, Western Geographical Series, Volume 11 (Victoria: Department of Geography, University of Victoria, 1975). In a series of seven essays, well-known geographers have documented their major investigations on aspects such as local manufacturing, the effects of the oil and natural gas industries and planning policies.

James G. MacGregor's *History of Alberta* (Edmonton: Hurtig Publishers, 1972) contains many references to Calgary, and the earlier *History of the Province of Alberta* (Calgary: The Western Canada Publishing

Company, 1912) by Dr. A.O. MacRae devotes considerable space to biographical sketches of early Calgarians. Students interested in comparative city studies are referred to Andrew T. Brown's *Frontier Community: Kansas City to 1870* (Columbia: University of Missouri Press, 1963); Alan F.J. Artibise's *Winnipeg: A Social History of Urban Growth, 1874-1914* (Montreal: McGill-Queen's University Press, 1975); and Artibise, *Winnipeg: An Illustrated History* (Toronto: James Lorimer and Co., 1977).

SPECIFIC THEMES

The Origins of Calgary

For more information on the whisky trade and the NWMP, the reader is directed to Paul Sharp's *Whoop-Up Country* (Minneapolis: University of Minnesota Press, 1955). This first-rate study gives an excellent background to the illegal whisky trade. The Mounted Police have received fairly close attention from historians. John Turner's *The North-West Mounted Police*, 2 Vols. (Ottawa: King's Printer, 1950) is still as good as any later published work with respect to the early days. A good complementary work is Hugh Dempsey, ed., *Men in Scarlet* (Calgary: Historical Society of Alberta and McClelland and Stewart West, 1974). This book contains many valuable articles on the Mounted Police, although special mention should be made of John Jenning's "The Plains Indian and the Law", an able comparison of the American and Canadian frontiers.

Hugh Dempsey has edited another book entitled *A Winter at Fort Macleod* (Calgary: McClelland and Stewart West, 1974). The bulk of this book contains the diary of R.V. Nevitt, one of the original members of the Mounted Police and an amateur artist who sketched Fort Calgary soon after its erection. Dempsey has also written an article on Inspector Ephrem Brisebois in the *Frontier Calgary* publication. Several members of the Mounted Police who had associations with Calgary have written their recollections. Cecil Denny wrote *The Riders of the Plains* (Calgary: Herald Printers, 1905) and *The Law Marches West* (Toronto: J.M. Dent, 1939). Sam Steele recorded his Calgary experiences in *Forty Years in Canada: Reminiscences of the Great North-West* (London: London and Norwich Press, 1915). R. Burton Deane, whose Calgary residence across from the old fort site is presently occupied by the Dandelion Gallery, wrote his reminiscences in a book called *Mounted Police Life in Canada* (London: Cassell and Co., 1916).

L.V. Kelly's *The Rangemen* (Toronto: William Briggs, 1913); Grant MacEwan's *Blazing the Old Cattle Trail* (Saskatoon: Modern Press, 1962); and G.M. MacInnes' *In the Shadow of the Rockies* (London: Rivingtons,

1930) probably give the best flavour of the early cattle industry in Alberta. Pierre Berton's second volume on the construction of the CPR, *The Last Spike* (Toronto: McClelland and Stewart, 1971) refers to the beginnings of Calgary. This readable book also provides a national perspective on the railway. A.S. Morton's monumental study, *A History of the Canadian West to 1870* (London: Thomas Nelson and Sons, 1939) is still the best reference on the early fur traders. J.K. Smith has prepared a short biography of *David Thompson* (Toronto: Oxford University Press, 1971). Finally, readers should consult Irene Spry's *The Palliser Expedition* (London: Macmillan and Co., 1964).

Economic Growth and Metropolitan Development

The writings of J.M.S. Careless, Canada's leading exponent of "metropolitanism" in history, are pertinent to this theme. His article, "Frontierism and Metropolitanism in Canadian History," *Canadian Historical Review*, XXXV, No. 1 (March 1954) should be examined in association with another Careless article, "Aspects of Urban Life in the West, 1870-1914," in G.A. Stelter and A.F.J. Artibise, eds., *The Canadian City: Essays in Urban History* (Toronto: McClelland and Stewart, 1977). Richard Wade's *The Urban Frontier* (Cambridge: Harvard University Press, 1959) and Gilbert Stelter's unpublished Ph.D. dissertation "The Urban Frontier: A Western Case Study, Cheyenne, Wyoming 1867-1887" (University of Alberta, 1968) provide good comparative studies.

A wealth of statistical data and maps is contained in Alberta government publications, to which the *Atlas of Alberta* (1969) is an invaluable companion. The *Alberta Industries and Resources* publications, which have appeared annually since the early 1970s, contain comparative statistics for Calgary dating back 50 years. Richard Baine has produced a booklet entitled *Calgary, An Urban Study*, Urban Study Series (Toronto: Clarke Irwin and Co., 1973). This volume has some very worthwhile visual material and also delineates specific fields for further enquiry.

Little published material exists on Calgary's economic development. Three articles in *Frontier Calgary* deal with aspects of urban economic development: J.P. Dickin McGinnes, "Birth to Boom to Bust: Building in Calgary 1875-1914"; Paul Voisey, "In Search of Wealth and Status: An Economic and Social Study of Entrepreneurs in Early Calgary"; and Max Foran, "Land Speculation and Urban Development in Calgary, 1884-1912".

The economic development of Calgary is loosely treated in two unpublished M.A. theses: L. Bussard, "Early History of Calgary" (University of Alberta, 1935) and D. Diller, "The Early Economic Development of Alberta Previous to 1905" (University of Alberta, 1930). In 1974, the Glenbow-Alberta Institute reprinted the 1885 edition of *Calgary, Alberta:*

Her Industries and Resources. The Historical Society of Alberta published *Calgary in Sandstone* in 1969. This booklet, prepared by Richard Cunniffe, provides good background on Calgary's first home-grown industry. M. Foran's "Urban Calgary, 1884-1895," *Histoire sociale/Social History*, Vol. V, No. 9 (April 1972) makes reference to the economic development of early Calgary. A good analysis of the ranching industry is contained in D.H. Breen's unpublished Ph.D. dissertation, "The Canadian West and the Ranching Frontier, 1875-1922" (University of Alberta, 1972). An article which deals specifically with the ranching industry and Calgary is L.G. Thomas' "The Rancher and the City: Calgary and the Cattlemen, 1883-1914," *Transactions of the Royal Society of Canada*, Vol. VI, Series IV, Section II (June 1968).

William Pearce and Pat Burns are the only two individuals vitally connected with the economic development of Calgary who have been the subject of academic studies. E.A. Mitchner has made an excellent study of William Pearce in a Ph.D. dissertation entitled "William Pearce, 1882-1904" (University of Alberta, 1971). Burns is treated in A.F. Sproule's M.A. thesis "The Role of Patrick Burns in the Economic Development of Western Canada" (University of Alberta, 1962).

For a good overview of the petroleum industry, see David H. Breen, "Calgary: The City and the Petroleum Industry Since World War Two," *Urban History Review*, No. 2-77 (October 1977), pp. 55-71. See also the libraries of the major oil companies for reports dealing with developments in the industry. A brief general history is George de Mille, *Oil in Canada West — The Early Years* (Calgary: North-West Printing and Lithographing, 1970). Some excellent thumbnail sketches of early oil pioneers can be found in James D. Hilborn, ed., *Dusters and Gushers* (Toronto: Pitt Publishing, 1968).

Population Growth and Ethnic Relationships

For material on ethnic groups refer to Artibise, *Western Canada Since 1870: A Select Bibliography and Guide* and B. Peel, *Bibliography of the Prairie Provinces to 1953*, 2nd. edition (Toronto: University of Toronto Press, 1973). J.S. Woodsworth's *Strangers Within Our Gates*, first published in 1909 and recently reprinted (Toronto: University of Toronto Press, 1972), gives a contemporary viewpoint of "the immigrant problem". Similarly, John Porter's *The Vertical Mosaic* (Toronto: University of Toronto Press, 1965) examines the modern period with respect to the assimilation of ethnic groups into a wider Canadian socio-economic structure. Howard Palmer offers a good survey on immigration to Alberta in his *Land of the Second Chance* (Lethbridge: *The Lethbridge Herald*, 1972). Palmer's "Nativism in Alberta" in *Historical Papers 1974*, published by the Canadian Historical Association, should also be consulted for the post-World War I period. J.E. Rea's article "The Roots of Prairie Society," in D. Gagan, ed., *Prairie Perspectives 1* (Toronto: Holt, Rinehart and Winston, 1970) discusses the Hartzian model as it applies to western Canadian society. Of interest also is J. Seedon, "Post-War Migration and the Canadian West: An Economic Analysis," in A.W. Rasporich and H.C. Klassen, eds., *Prairie Perspectives 2* (Toronto: Holt, Rinehart and Winston, 1973).

The Chinese community has been studied by G.A. Baureiss in his M.A. thesis "The City and the Sub-Community: The Chinese of Calgary" (University of Calgary, 1971). J. Brian Dawson's article in *Frontier Calgary*, "The Chinese Experience in Frontier Calgary, 1885-1910", also contains some good information and should be consulted along with Baureiss' thesis. References to the various ethnic groups are also found in the *Century Calgary* series. The *Alberta Historical Review* has featured articles on various immigrant groups in the province. Typical of these are the two contained in the summer 1976 edition, "Scandinavian Homesteaders" by William Wonders and "The Japanese in Southern Alberta, 1941-45" by David Iwaasa.

There is little published information available on Calgary's population. In 1959, Professor P.J. Smith prepared for the City of Calgary Planning Department a *Study of Calgary's Past and Probable Future Population Growth*. Smith has also written two articles, "Calgary, A Study in Urban Patterns," *Economic Geography*, Vol. 38 (October 1962) and "Change in a Youthful City: The Case of Calgary, Alberta," *Geography*, Vol. 56 (January 1971).

The Urban Landscape

The most concentrated selection of material on Calgary's physical growth is contained in the library of the City of Calgary Planning Department. Most of this material is devoted to the modern period, but reference is made to historical precedents. There is a host of transportation studies and there are copies of every urban scheme undertaken by the city since 1950. Some relevant theses have also addressed themselves to particular aspects of urban development. Four of the more interesting unpublished M.A. theses are by J.F. Crabbe, "Retail Stores' Spatial Affinities in the Central Business District, Calgary, Alberta" (Queen's University, 1972); H.L. Diemer, "Annexation and Amalgamation in the Territorial Growth of Edmonton and Calgary" (University of Alberta, 1974); D.G. Harasym, "Planning of New Residential Areas in Calgary, 1944-73" (University of Alberta, 1975); and R. Peddie, "Urban Parks and Planning in Calgary" (University of Calgary, 1968).

A discussion of the townsite controversy is contained in M. Foran's "Early Calgary, 1875-1895: The Controversy Surrounding the Townsite Location and the Direction of Town Expansion," in A.R. McCormack and I. MacPherson, eds., *Cities in the West: Papers of the Western Canadian Urban History Conference* (Ottawa: National Museum of Man, Mercury Series, 1975). Thomas Mawson's original report on city planning is located in the Glenbow Archives. The report was published as *The City of Calgary: Past, Present, and Future* under the auspices of the City Planning Commission of Calgary and may be available in various public libraries. An excellent discussion of land development and usage in Canada with particular reference to Calgary is Peter Spurr's *Land and Urban Development: A Preliminary Study* (Toronto: James Lorimer and Co., 1976).

The Urban Community: Society and Politics

For general material on politics, the reader should consult C.B. Macpherson, *Democracy in Alberta: Social Credit and the Party System* (Toronto: University of Toronto Press, 1953). L.P.V. Johnson and Ola MacNutt's *Aberhart of Alberta* (Edmonton: Institute of Applied Art Ltd., 1970) provides insights into this fascinating political figure. A history of the farm movement in Alberta is contained in N. Priestly and E. Swindlehurst's *Furrows, Faith and Fellowship* (Edmonton: Co-op Press Ltd., 1967). George Stanley's article on R.B. Bennett in *Frontier Calgary* should be read for information on Bennett's Calgary days. Denis Smith's article in *Prairie Perspectives 1*, "Liberals and Conservatives on the Prairies, 1917-1968", describes the rather unique political character of western Canada. Carl Betke discusses the relationship between labour and the UFA in "Farm Politics in an Urban Age: The Decline of the United Farmers of Alberta after 1921," in L.H. Thomas, ed., *Essays on Western History* (Edmonton: University of Alberta Press, 1976).

For information on local government, readers are directed to Eric Hanson, *Local Government in Alberta* (Toronto: McClelland and Stewart, 1956). Local government in Calgary is discussed more specifically in M. Foran's M.A. thesis, "The Calgary Town Council, 1884-1895: A Study of Local Government in a Frontier Environment" (University of Calgary, 1970). Readers are also directed to Foran's "The Travis Affair," *Alberta Historical Review* (Summer 1973) and his "Bob Edwards and Social Reform," *Alberta Historical Review* (Autumn 1971). Edwards is the subject of a biography by Grant MacEwan in *Eye Opener Bob* (Edmonton: Institute of Applied Art, 1957). Hugh Dempsey has also edited a collection of Edwards' most memorable writings in *The Best of Bob Edwards* (Edmonton: Hurtig Publishers, 1975).

There are no histories of Calgary utilities except for Grant MacEwan's article on Calgary Power published by that company in the early 1960s.

However, Calgary figures prominently in Tony Cashman's history of the Alberta Government Telephones, *Singing Wires* (Edmonton: A.G.T., 1972). A history of the Calgary police force appears in the *Century Calgary* series. Robert Stamp has prepared a very readable history of the Calgary Public School Board in *School Days, A Century of Memories* (Calgary: McClelland and Stewart West, 1975). This book, part of the school board's centenary project, accounts for the growth of education in Calgary since 1885. N.L. McLeod's Ph.D. dissertation, "Calgary College, 1912-1915: A Study of an Attempt to Establish a Privately Financed University in Calgary" (University of Calgary, 1970) is also useful.

H.C. Klassen's two articles, "Life in Frontier Calgary," in A.W. Rasporich, ed., *Western Canada Past and Present* (Calgary, 1975) and "Social Troubles in Calgary in the Mid-1890's," *Urban History Review*, No. 3-74 (February 1974), should be consulted. Klassen's article in *Frontier Calgary*, "The *Bond of Brotherhood* and Calgary Workingmen", should be read in conjunction with E. Taraska's M.A. thesis, "The Calgary Craft Union Movement, 1900-1920 (University of Calgary, 1975). The churches are covered adequately in the *Century Calgary* series. Two books which deal with the growth of churches are V. Byrne's *From the Buffalo to the Cross* (Calgary, 1973) and Rev. David J. Carter's *Where the Wind Blows: A History of the Anglican Diocese of Calgary* (Calgary, 1968).

There are many monographs, reminiscences and other pertinent articles on Calgary's history in the Glenbow collection. M. Foran has prepared a bibliography on some of the most useful of these sources for the Calgary Board of Education's Social Studies Department. Readers are also directed to the Glenbow's extensive photograph collection and to the Glenbow's recent acquisition of approximately 900 linear feet of papers from the City Clerk's Department. As yet largely uncatalogued, these papers should provide a wealth of additional information on many aspects of municipal policy-making and related matters.

Index

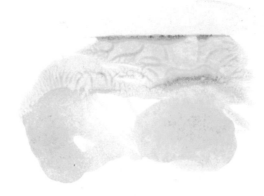